MUSIC FOR LIFE
The Salani Brothers

By Barbara Salani

To Veronika,

hoping this book will inspire you,

Happy Holidays

Love,

Barbara Salani

Copyright © 2017 by Barbara Salani
All rights reserved. This book or any portion thereof may not be reproduced or used in any manner whatsoever without the express written permission of the publisher except for the use of brief quotations in a book review.

Printed in the United States of America

First Printing, 2017

ISBN-13: 978-1981172184
ISBN-10: 1981172181

Barbara Salani
2231 N. Conference Dr.
Boca Raton, Florida 33486

www.4loveofmusic.com

Acknowledgments

I would like to thank all those who contributed to this biography: Renato Salani for his Diary and all his interviews together with Giulio Salani, Nullo Viti, Laura Helman, Daniele Giannini, Adriano Salani, Andrea Salani, Mario Gragnani, Leonardo Salani for information related to the topic, and Stephano Daniel Salani for his legal guidance. Many thanks to Jessica Salani and to my son Gregory Albiani for modifying all the countless pictures included in the book.
Appreciation for Rebecca Noble and DigDev, who made a fundamental contribution to the graphic design of the book cover and the creation of the website: I thank you wholeheartedly.
Gratitude to Lauren Overzet who corrected the drafts and edited with dedication and professionalism. Appreciation for Karen Noble's and Teresa Stenson's contribution as well.

Special thanks also to my cousin Stefano Salani, Music Engineer, for restoring the songs performed by Renato Salani's Orchestra, and making them in digital format, suitable for publication along with this book on the website: www.4loveofmusic.com

To my brother, Sergio Salani, thank you for believing in me, for encouraging me to pursue this family project, and for always being there for me. Above all, I would like to thank my Aunt Alma with all my heart for being of fundamental help in the reconstruction of stories, for adding information regarding the order of events, for providing photos and essential material for documenting facts, and for dedicating so much of her time to help me.

To everyone:
THANK YOU SO MUCH!
I am eternally grateful.

Here are some members of the Salani Family Project: (From left to right) Alma, Renato, Barbara, Sergio and Giulio.

The Author with the main characters of the book: Renato on the left, and Giulio on the right.

PREFACE

I dedicate this book to my father Giulio, and to my Uncle Renato, for whom MUSIC played a key role throughout their lives. Special men, full of talent and great human goodness, capable of many sacrifices without complaint, and always thanking God for giving them the most precious gifts: good health, their family love, and the good fortune to be able to rejoice in contemplating the beauty of life.

My father is currently 92 years old and, unfortunately, he suffers from Alzheimer's. However, when I remind him of the vicissitudes he went through during the war, all the sufferings he experienced in those times are engraved in his memory—in the depths of his soul—and he still remembers many details. This book talks about him and the many things he taught me. A lesson I learned from my father is that there is no truer truth than the one a man gets through music.

Back when his memories were crystal clear, I asked him, "Dad, what do you want me to say in this book from you?" He replied, " I want everyone to remember me as a genuine and honest man."

What is the purpose of life? To live happily, to enjoy the little beautiful things nature has to offer and good health allows us to see, and to rejoice in the smallest of achievements, while not being discouraged in the most difficult of times. For this, MUSIC is the remedy to help us make a more pleasant journey through life.

The other star of these pages is my Uncle Renato. His DIARY (together with some live interviews in various locations and the materials I've collected during four years of research) is the main source of the stories I'm about to describe.

Renato Salani's DIARY began in 1944 when he arrived as a prisoner at the Fossoli Concentration Camp, a place located a few miles from Carpi (Modena, Italy) a Nazi prison camp for Jewish and political prisoners.

He decided to write his DIARY in ancient Italian, in a language that reminds us of the "Florentine vulgar", the mother of the Italian language. Although freely, Renato was inspired by Dante Alighieri's masterwork the *Divine Comedy* and he wrote his poem in quatrains of hendecasyllable verses, differentiating his *Diary* from Dante's which was composed by tercets of hendecasyllable verses.

Why this choice? Maybe because Uncle Renato, like the great poet, was beginning a long journey into hell, not Dante's imaginary and metaphorical *Inferno*, but the real hell of captivity. Perhaps he thought the beauty and musicality of hendecasyllable verses were the best antidote to the barbarism he was experiencing—a way to preserve his dignity and hope.

> *Oh, my dear Muse who dictates me*
> *the few verses I'll be composing.*
> *I will try to go narrating*
> *the painful story of these poor people.*

I must point out that Renato's poems were written with a typewriter on TOILET PAPER from the concentration camp. My Aunt Alma, Renato's wife, kept and guarded these scraps like one would guard a relic, so that now, after more than seventy years, this "relic" can be brought to light, given to the prints, and shared with you - a story of two special men and a fragment of our recent history.

This is the task I have undertaken.

In this book, some words are capitalized. It is a desired choice, a recall to the *Leitmotiv* of Richard Wagner's Operas. These are key words, recurring in the narration, which constitute a characterizing feature. These words were the spark that kindled in me the desire, almost the need to write this book, and have fueled the passion with which I wrote it. I hope this spark of interest will be ignited within you, the reader, and that these repeated, capitalized words will keep that flame of interest and involvement alight.

Here are some verses written on the TOILET PAPER piece that is shown in the photo:

*[...] when one night a bomb comes to us;
oh, what a general fright!!!*

*A scream both outside and in, everyone
hiding, under the bunk-beds.
A hiss ... and then that bare light -
the shot.... words cannot express our fear.*

*Everyone, I'm certain, believed
in that moment, something had fallen upon them.
But then in each heart, I'm sure they prayed
that the good Lord had not sent it.*

*But then you see yourself out of the glow,
and we all go to the door ...
Our heartbeats, strong, as we look upon
those whose souls were taken beside us.*

*"Pippo" * had thrown a piece
on the command of the camp nearby
and hit the mark right where
it wanted, what an unbearable feeling.*

*In a few words, this was the result:
three dead and three injured among the Germans.
Lea finished on a wire fence full of thorns
hurting her knee with arabesques.*

* During the final stages of the Second World War, "Pippo" was the name that was popularly given to night-fighter airplanes in Northern Italy. "Pippo" airplanes came flying very close to the ground, to avoid anti-aircraft artillery, throwing bombs into the darkness of the night. The actions were made possible by the first installations of radar equipment on airplanes, had been scheduled by the Allies with the complex operation called "Night Intruder" and was entrusted to RAF pilots.

quando a un tratto ecco che ci arriva
una bomba: Oh che spavento generale!!!

Un urlo fuori e dentro tutti sotto
i castelletti andammo poi a finire.-
Un sibilo... e la luce via di botto,
il colpo.... non ti so la fifa dire.-

Ognuno senza dubbio s'aspettava
che sul capo qualcosa gli cascasse;
Ma poi in cuor suo son certo che pregava
perché il buon Dio non glielo mandasse.

Ma poi si veden fuori dei bagliori
e tutti andiamo ansanti sulla porta
Si sente forte il battito dei cuori
di quei che a noi vicino han l'alma morta

Attento aveva "Pippo" una spezzone
sul Comando del Campo qui vicino
e colto ha proprio in quella direzione
in che voleva colpire il birichino.

Insomma questo è stato il risultato:
Tre morti e tre feriti fra i tedeschi,
la Lea finita su un reticolato
s'è fatta ad un ginocchio dei rabeschi.

THE SALANI FAMILY TREE
Only with the characters mentioned in the book:

In Brazil   *In Italy*

Gesualda & Franceschini   Luigi & Maria

Maria Franceschini   Euclide, Arduino

Maria & Euclide Salani

Elsa, Olga, Ada e Renato

In Italy

Gesualda & Giulio Meneghetti

Maria & Euclide   Raimondo & Mario

Elsa, Olga, Ada, Renato and Giulio

Renato & Alma   -   Giulio & Nancy

In Venezuela and later in the USA.

Renato & Alma   Giulio & Nancy

Stefano, Riccardo & Andrea - Leonardo, Barbara & Sergio

Chapter 1
PARENTS IN BRAZIL

My grandmother Maria (Renato and Giulio's mother) was a tall woman—attractive, beautiful, and strong, with a very sweet face enlightened by pale blue eyes. She was also a devoted mother, who loved her children very much and gave her love in abundance. My father tells me that during the war when the food was rationed, Grandma Maria would selflessly give some of her food to the kids, claiming that she was not hungry. She wished to make their rations more plentiful saying, "they need more nourishment to grow." As a result, she lost a lot of weight, yet she never complained; her lips were always graced with a smile. My father recalls a vivid memory of her in a sleek blue coat—her stylish and refined figure had changed so much that she now looked like a very elegant woman. She was a mere 45 kilos (99 pounds) then.

Grandma Maria was born in Brazil to Gesualda and Franceschini, but when her father got sick, they all moved back to Italy.

After Franceschini's death, her mother married a friend of her late husband, Giulio Meneghetti. He was a good man from the village of Massaciuccoli. Meneghetti had a passion for fishing and hunting, and often met Maestro Giacomo Puccini (the famous composer living in Torre del Lago) in the middle of Massaciuccoli Lake. Together, they practiced and cultivated their favorite passion: hunting.

Feeling nostalgic for her country of birth, Grandma Maria returned to Brazil to live with her uncle, Franceschini's brother, who had a tailoring shop in São Paulo. During the time she was already a pretty young lady, helping her uncle in his custom clothing store, she met Euclide Salani. They fell in love, became engaged, and after a few years, they got married.

Euclide was born in San Martino Spino, in the province of Modena, where the Salanis had been known for generations as the "bell ringers". This nickname dates back to 1850, when Gioacchino Salani was commissioned by a priest to carry out the duties of the sacristan, as well as the bell ringer. This assignment was passed from father to son and remained in the Salani family, until 1945.

During his youth, Euclide lived in the house of his Aunt Maria and his Uncle Luigi, who was the bell-ringer of his town. Maria and Luigi loved Euclide and raised him as their own, along with their son, Arduino. Euclide was the first of the Salanis to try out different musical instruments besides the bells—in fact, as a child, he began to study music, revealing a talent worthy of being cultivated. For this reason, he decided to enroll at the Conservatory of Bologna. While he was studying, he also taught music to the children of the wealthiest families of the town and conducted the San Martino Spino Municipal Band for a short time.

An interesting anecdote is that while Euclide practiced the piano during the evenings, Arduino would hide under the piano to listen to him play. Euclide normally didn't want anyone to listen to him while he practiced, but he pretended not to notice when his little cousin was hiding. The bond between the two of them became incredibly strong—stronger even than one between brothers.

Even though he was still a boy, Euclide decided to leave for Brazil, driven by the desire to go out and "chase his dream". In São Paulo, he worked in the liqueur factory of another uncle, enabling him to earn money and support himself while keeping up with his studies.

He had a double belt where he kept the gold *marenghi* (Italian golden collector's coins, which at that time represented a secure investment), and when the belt was full, he secured passage on a ship heading for Italy.

Upon his arrival, he rode a bicycle from San Martino Spino to the Conservatory of Bologna to take exams as an orchestra conductor. After a few years of traveling from São Paulo to Bologna, he finally earned his diploma. The euphonium was his primary instrument, but he wrote band arrangements with his secondary instrument, the piano. All of his scores were written by hand—not mass printed—and yet they were often confused with prints, as he had such immaculate handwriting.

Euclide continued on to become the conductor of a band, and during every holiday he led performances of many of his own arrangements at the central plaza of Ribeirão Preto. In fact, during a recent move, I found manuscripts of these performances in my aunt's attic, written by Euclide himself. I was able to go back and read through all the scores he conducted with that band, as well as the arrangements he made for each instrument. The band's repertoire ranged from symphonic to opera, along with some songs from the Carnival of Viareggio.

Among the scores I found were: symphonies by Brahms, Beethoven, and Schubert; Gioacchino Rossini's *The Barber of Seville*; *L'Elisir d'Amore* by Gaetano Donizetti; *La Gioconda* by Amilcare Ponchielli; and Euclide's own compositions for his band, based on famous operas, entitled *Concerted Piece from the Opera La Traviata* by Giuseppe Verdi, *Fantasy on the Opera La Bohème* by Giacomo Puccini, *Cavalleria Rusticana* by Pietro Mascagni, *Agnus Dei, Religious Melody* by Georges Bizet, *Faust* by Charles Gounod, *Athalia* by Felix Mendelssohn, and many more.

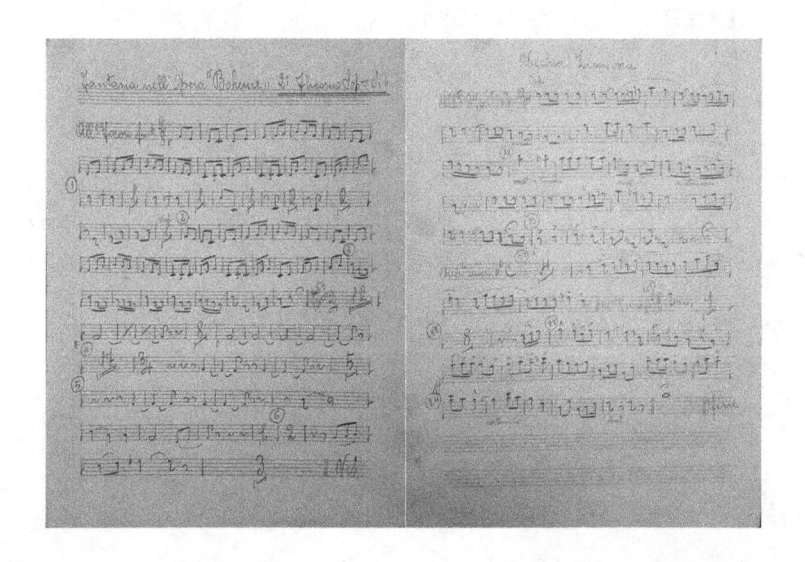

I Photo of Euclide Salani's manuscripts of the *Fantasy on the Opera La Boheme* inspired by Giacomo Puccini's opera, arrangement for the 2nd Flugelhorn Soprano in B♭, and next *Vecchia Zimarra* for 1st Euphonium.

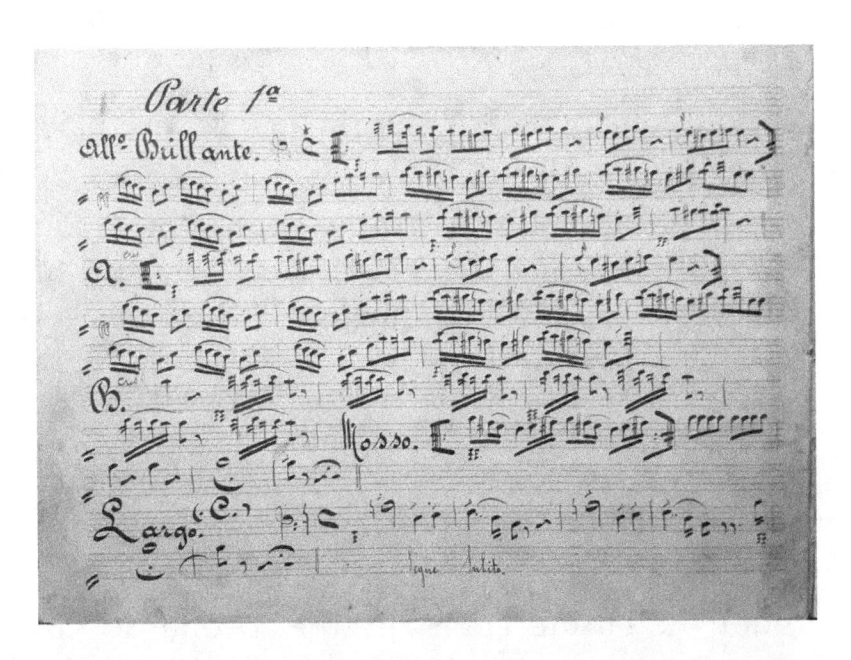

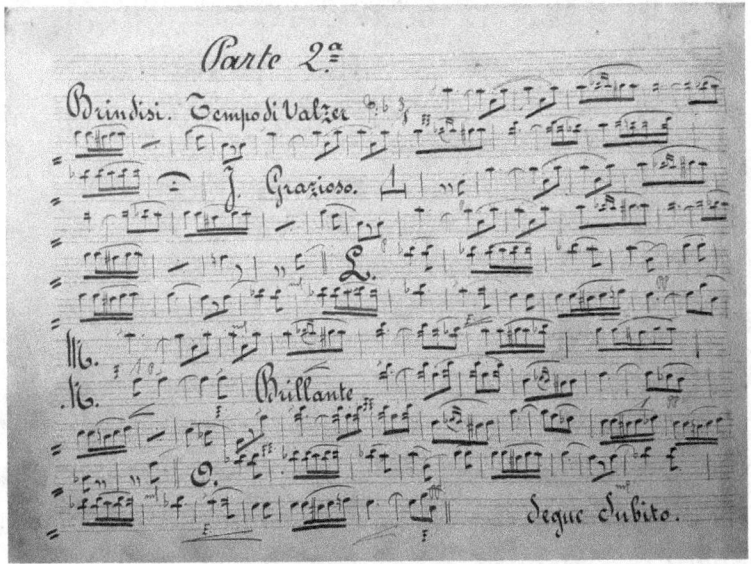

Photo of the *Concerted Piece from the Opera La Traviata* for 1st Principal Clarinet in B♭, arranged and hand written by Maestro Euclide Salani, inspired by Giuseppe Verdi's opera.

Not only was Euclide passionate about music, but he also loved the Italian language, traditions, and culture. At the beginning of the twentieth century, he and other expatriates of the Italian colony established in São Paulo realized the need to create a teaching institute dedicated to preserving their culture. On July 9th, 1911, they founded the Italo-Brazilian institute, Dante Alighieri, and on February 17th, 1913, sixty pupils began their studies under Italian teachers in the Leonardo da Vinci building. Traditional and yet also a modernist vanguard, the institute already showed its innovative spirit by accepting students of both sexes.

Euclide and Maria's marriage was a difficult one. Not only were they very far apart in age, they also had extremely different personalities. Maria was good and simple; she was not highly educated, but she loved her family and was always trying to please everyone. Euclide, on the other hand, was authoritarian, short-tempered, and grumpy, yet he was very fond of culture and music.

Euclide and Maria had five children: three girls, Elsa, Olga and Ada, and two boys, Renato and Giulio. The first four children were born in San Simon, Brazil. Renato, the first boy after the three girls, was celebrated as a king. From here comes his name: RE (king in Italian) and NATO (born). Renato: The King Is Born. This king was born on September 23rd, 1922.

This photo, taken before Renato's birth, was the Salani home in Brazil. You can see Euclide standing on the sidewalk, very elegant with his black suit, tie, and hat. Close to him his two older daughters Elsa and Olga, while baby Ada is sitting on the window held by Maria. You can also see their neighbors' family, who are all posing with the Salanis.

After Renato's birth, the family moved to Ribeirão Preto, a fraction of Sao Paulo, to live near Euclide's liqueur factory. On every festive occasion in the village square, Euclide led the band performing many of his arrangements.

Here we see the Salani family in front of their home in Ribeirão Preto, going for a ride in their relative's car. There's Euclide at the back, with the mustache, and a relative is driving the car.

The Salani Family inside their home in Brazil.

When Renato was three years old, and his sisters were already beautiful young ladies, the entire Salani family moved to Italy. The decision was made especially for the safety of the daughters. At that time, in Brazil, men would break into homes at night to seize girls for various ill purposes—rape, prostitution, and even slavery were not uncommon—so the Salanis felt Italy would be a safer place for their daughters.

Euclide decided to sell the liquor factory and all the properties to a friend, with the intention of returning to Italy as soon as they were able.

From left to right: Olga, Elsa, and Ada.

Chapter 2
ARRIVAL IN ITALY

Grandfather Euclide came to Italy with a considerable amount of money gained from the sale of his liquor factory in Brazil. He would have been able to invest this large sum of money in real estate, but Maria's stepbrother, Raimondo (Giulio Meneghetti's and Gesualda's son), asked Euclide for a loan to expand his grocery business. Raimondo assured him it was a good investment and that he would return the money with interest. Euclide was a good man and confident in Raimondo's word, so he gave him all the money he possessed, believing he would receive all that money back, and more.

Unfortunately, that didn't happen. Raimondo didn't return a lira, even when Renato and Giulio went to him and asked for food from his store. They waited all day long, and would have gone home empty-handed, if it hadn't been for their Uncle Mario (brother and partner of Raimondo) sneaking them some groceries.

When the Salani family arrived in Italy, Maria was pregnant with my father, Giulio. She gave birth two months later at Massaciuccoli in the house of her mother's new husband, her adoptive father's home. His name was Giulio Meneghetti, whom my father was named after.

Maria, daughter of the deceased Franceschini and Gesualda, inherited from her father a house in Via Pisana in the Varignano district of Viareggio. After Giulio's birth, on October 2nd, 1925, she and her whole family moved in and lived there for many years. Renato and Giulio shortly began studying music with their father, the former maestro of the Municipal Band in Viareggio. Euclide had many students, and on several occasions Renato and Giulio helped him teach the beginners. The two brothers also had to be able to play all the instruments in the band, so they could substitute for any musicians who were absent.

The Band conducted by Maestro Euclide Salani, parading in Viareggio in front of the Burlamacca Canal. The youngest is Renato playing the clarinet.

To rebuild the atmosphere of the Salani home in those years, let Uncle Renato's poetry speak for itself, giving us a colorful description of his father while rethinking about his own childhood:

My dad, Euclide Salani's words: Shut up!
When you speak to me, you must be silent!
Don't make mistakes or you'll be in trouble;
think only about doing your duty.

Only your duty is not enough,
you must do more and more;

*there is no time to wander idly,
no time to play Canasta - or any other game.*

*Long is the way but life is short,
time is not useless.
When you have learnt all you can from science,
you will all live more peacefully.*

*So, stop! Do not get up!
Do not move after eating your meal:
you, Maria, clean up the dishes and cutlery and
you, Elsa, bring Renato's books,*

*Giulio's, Ada's, Olga's books,
help them with their homework;
ensure that their professor will not fail them
for any misunderstandings.*

*You, Renato, must play the piano,
so, try not to fool around,
your hands must be fast and ready
for your teacher's discerning eye.*

Maestro Euclide Salani.

So, this story was repeated
every day we spent on God's earth.
Reveling was forbidden:
for I always had to be ready for war.

I had to rush and apprize in a hurry
all the musicians of the band's service;
switching from trombone to trumpet
whenever a player was missing.

This was my permanent duty;
did I have time for the raids?
I found freedom running to the "Renaio"(sandpit)
with my friends
to go bathing without underpants.

Still a few lines on my father
to concentrate his essence in a few words:
a precise, fussy man, he instilled fear with a glance
and placed demands on his worried children.

He got a degree in Bologna as a conductor,
and played the euphonium like a God.
He could play other instruments if needed.
In the privacy of home, he loved to drink wine.

He understood clarinets, flutes, and flugelhorns,
knew all about carpentry,
he built an oven at the back of the garden,
and considered being a shoemaker.

He was a modest but omniscient man;
I think he was too good.
In our house, though - no, not so much.
His intimidating voice was like thunder.

Only now I understand why,
as I find myself treading in his footsteps:
and the more I understand him,
the more I recognize he was enormous.

*No, I do not forget he was severe,
he lived in a bitter and lonely way;
a truly strong character,
an extremely authoritarian man.*

*When we were kids, we thought he didn't like us,
we could not enter into his world;
now, yes, we can understand
his illusion ... his deep love.*

*Thanks, Dad, for the morality,
which you instilled in my heart;
I tried to be faithful to the primal promise:
elevating our surname high ... in your honor.*

The band parade in the Pineta, Viareggio. Once again, the youngest is Renato.

*At the age of eight years old,
I started playing the quarter size clarinet in the band:
I was a little kid and a bit overweight,
walking and performing was a problem for me.*

In this photo, Uncle Renato is playing the euphonium, and you can see my Grandfather Euclide facing his band. As I mentioned earlier, if one band member was missing, Renato and Giulio had to be able to play the instrument of any missing musician.

Uncle Renato with his quarter size clarinet, wearing the band's uniform in front of his house in Viareggio. From the window seen in the picture above, came the notes and MUSIC the Salani boys played.

Euclide Salani is located in the center of the picture among the members of his band: Giulio is the third from the left, under the "G" and Renato is the fourth from the right, under the "R".

The years went by; and when Renato and Giulio were teenagers, friends, neighbors, and acquaintances stopped willingly outside the window of their modest home and often asked them to play famous pieces and songs of the time. The brothers performed with great enthusiasm, and were happy to play both popular songs, as well as much more demanding musical works. My uncle performed De Falla's *Fire Dance*, *The Flight of the Bumblebee* by Rimsky-Korsakov, and *Warsaw Concerto* by Addinsell, while my father played Strauss, Fritz Kreisler's most famous compositions, and more on the violin.

While his children were learning and playing, Euclide worked hard teaching music lessons, writing arrangements, composing music, and conducting the band. However, payments from the city of Viareggio for his performances were a struggle to collect. Although he protested and they promised, the payments never came when they were supposed to.

At that time, Uncle Renato was taking piano lessons with Maestro Leonardo Pacini, a Capuchin friar of the Church of San Francesco in Viareggio.

Padre Pacini was a great master with an infinite amount of patience and the capacity to teach his students with much passion and love. As a composer and a conductor, he was highly appreciated, and, as testament to his talent, he was recommended as a music teacher by the great composer Giacomo Puccini to students in the area.

In 1921, Padre Pacini founded the first Viareggio music school dedicated to Benedetto Marcello: a composer, writer, and poet who lived during the late Baroque period in Venice. Sadly, because of his delicate health, Padre Pacini had to abandon his teaching. When he died, it was a huge blow to Uncle Renato, who suffered greatly from his absence.

To this day, the city of Viareggio still remembers Padre Pacini as an important animator of Viareggio's cultural life.

Uncle Renato wrote these lines in memory of Padre Pacini:

What a holy man, what a dear Master:
I cherish in my mind his advice.
Those days when I feel a little insecure,
I appeal to his teachings and apply them.

While Renato was studying with Padre Pacini, Giulio was taking violin lessons from a well-known Maestro in Viareggio. An interesting side note: Renato paid the five liras for Giulio's first lesson out of his own pocket.

The Salani brothers went to school at the Istituto Suore Santa Marta - De Sortis, at Varignano, a district of Viareggio. It was run by nuns, both as orphanage and as elementary school, and was located near their home. Uncle Renato was very fond of his teacher, Sister Angela, and my father was very fond of his, Sister Barbara. My father and Sister Barbara developed a very deep mutual affection, and so when I was born, he named me Barbara in her honor.

Years later, on vacation in Viareggio with my parents, my father introduced me to my namesake. I had heard stories told about her so affectionately that I was thrilled to see her in person!

She was so small, so delicate, and she still remembered my father Giulio very well, even after all those years. She knew my parents had given me her name and spoke to me so sweetly and tenderly—De Sortis Santa Marta sisters have always loved all children and held a great resource of affection for the Salani brothers!

Chapter 3
CHILDREN WORKING AT GATTO NERO.

Today, children playing at the *pineta* (pinewood park) in Viareggio visit the Gatto Nero snack bar to have a taste of its famous, exquisite donuts filled with cream, Nutella, or various ice cream flavors. Before World War II, the Gatto Nero was a ballroom attended by tourists, celebrities, and holiday entrepreneurs on vacation in Viareggio and the surrounding areas. As young boys, Renato and Giulio worked there during the summers as cigarette and cigar vendors, earning a wage to help their family.

Renato, three years older than his brother, was the first to take up his post at the Gatto Nero when he was just eight years old. Concerned that Giulio, who was only five, might get lost in the pinewood park, Renato took him to the movies while he worked his four-hour shift. On one occasion, Giulio saw the same movie multiple times while waiting for his brother to finish work.

Here in his diary, Renato recalls taking Giulio to the movies before going to work in the afternoons:

When I was a kid I was working
at Gatto Nero as a cigar vendor,
and I took Giulio to the cinema by bike
to watch the same movie several times.

Leaving from work in the evening,
I'd hold him as he perched on the frame of my bike,
and he would retell the whole movie,
on our way home, before supper and rest.

"Starting off on the right foot"
The refrain says, and this is the reality:
Giulio sold his games as a child,
just to buy a cigar for daddy.

He would run to get fresh water from the fountain,
would run to the bakery shop,
trying to make life easy.
He ran everywhere; he ran to avoid problems.

In the band, he started playing the piccolo,
then he had my same destiny:

to change a hundred instruments, but the clarinet accompanied him along his way.

Giulio at eight years old as a cigar vendor at Gatto Nero.

(Left) Renato at ten years old. (Right) Renato wearing his Gatto Nero cigar vendor uniform.

Renato, however, was not born to sell cigarettes in swanky ballrooms to wealthy aristocrats. To succeed, one must be a little shameless in order to attract a customer's attention and snatch up large tips. Renato was not like that. He was too shy to accept tips and even begged the waiters to go in his place and deliver cigarettes to his customers. As such, his earnings were meager.

Mr. Chilosi, the owner of the ballroom, realized he needed to change Renato's job in order to help him. He noticed this shy boy's eagerness to work, so he appointed him to be an assistant bartender.

Renato embraced his new job with great gusto, but one evening, the pianist of the live orchestra resigned, having received the call for his military duty. Mr. Chilosi, finding himself without a pianist in the middle of peak season, did not delay one second. He knew Renato played the piano, so he asked him to replace the outgoing pianist. Renato took off his black tie as a bartender and donned a black bow tie as a member of the orchestra.

*This way, I spoke with Mr. Chilosi,
who was called Carlino,
and he sent me to play the piano for his famous customers.
My neck tie became a bow tie:
my transformation was complete.*

*I was fourteen or maybe younger,
filled with enthusiasm and also fear,
For those gentlemen in the audience did not stop
requesting complicated musical pieces.*

*I don't think I played too many of those songs,
knowing how shy I was;
but I was encouraged and appreciated,
as I started my musical career.*

*Little by little my horizons opened,
the greatest unknowns disappeared:
my hands and fingers were getting ready
to play with agility and command.*

Renato Salani at 14, playing the piano with the Gatto Nero orchestra.

The Gatto Nero nightclub was open only during the summer, so Renato had to find another job during the other seasons. By the age of 14, he was a well-rounded musician, conducting, as well as arranging and performing, in an orchestra of forty musicians at the former Pacini Theater in Viareggio (which later was destroyed by bombs during World War II).

His friends considered him a prodigy, and this thought was fuelled and confirmed by the time he appeared on stage playing two instruments simultaneously: his right hand playing the trumpet and his left hand accompanying on the piano. He attracted everyone's attention and the theater erupted in thunderous applause when he finished.

One day, the audience were aroused in fever and passion.
The people, standing, very close to one another,
they applauded me with great heat,
because I played the piano and the trumpet together.

Nevertheless, his father, Euclide, was never a member of the ecstatic audience. He was a very severe and apprehensive father, who never participated in his son's performances. Maybe he didn't attend because he was modest, and abounding praise made him uneasy, or maybe he was afraid of making a social gaffe. No one knows.

Chapter 4
WORLD WAR II

Giulio was only 14 years old and Renato 17 when the Second World War broke out in 1939. They were both attending a junior accounting school at the *Istituto Superiore di Istruzione Carlo Piaggia* in Viareggio. Their father, Euclide, did not want his children's cultural experiences to be limited to music, so he urged them to study further. With junior degrees in accounting, he believed they would be able to better handle every situation in life.

When Renato was 18, he was called to enlist in La Spezia Italian Navy, and as a consequence he was forced to quit his studies. Despite this, Renato was still able to use his great musical skills and talent in this new chapter of his life. After some time at the naval base, he was transferred to Rome to join the Italian Navy Orchestra.

*In those frantic days, I became a soldier;
the end was coming.
I was sent to Rome to play in the Orchestra.
All our fleet was going wrecked.*

My uncle told me about the day he arrived at the naval base in Rome: he submitted his papers and credentials at the admissions office and explained that he had been transferred from La Spezia to Rome to take the pianist's place in the Italian Navy Orchestra. The employees examined his documents and handed over some tools, but they were not what Renato was expecting—a bucket, a brush, a broom, and a rag! To his dismay they said, "All right, all right! Now you have to clean the floors, then wash the stairs and the bathrooms ... "

Fortunately, as Uncle Renato began to protest, the commander passed by and heard him. When asked what the problem was, Uncle Renato responded, "I'm Renato Salani and I was transferred to Rome from La Spezia to replace the orchestra pianist, but if they make me clean the floors, they will ruin my hands and I will no longer be able to play."

The commander ordered Renato to follow him to his office where he gave him a test of his typing skills. Satisfied with the result, the commander told him to report to him the next day as his secretary, at least until the director of the orchestra called him.

The call came soon, so Uncle Renato did not have to do paperwork for long. Renato was now part of the orchestra of the Italian Navy, and was sent to military bases all over Italy to boost the morale of soldiers who had to leave for the front.

The Orchestra of the Italian Navy with Renato Salani at the piano. (On the right)

The orchestra was part of a show company with which several artists performed, including the comedian Ugo Tognazzi (a well-admired performer, director, and screenwriter, who went on to star in many famous films), as well as singer Lucio Ardenzi (a renowned singer and actor, who later became one of the most prestigious entrepreneurs of Italian theater companies). During the Second World War, they committed themselves to make varied shows for their fellow soldiers.

Renato in the center, among other musicians of the Orchestra of the Navy, which performed throughout Italy. Here, they are in Florence.

Renato Salani in Venice before performing with the Italian Orchestra of the Navy.

Photo dedicated to Renato by Ugo Tognazzi during a show: "To my friend Salani wishing to work again with you very soon, Ugo Tognazzi".

While his brother was off serving in the war, Giulio was busy studying accounting. Thanks to the help of his three older sisters (who had already graduated), Giulio managed to work ahead in his classes and skip one academic year, allowing him to have the option of graduating ahead of time.

Giulio (left) and Renato (right), when Renato was still in the Navy, on the promenade of their hometown, Viareggio.

When Renato came home and started back at school, he found himself in the same class as his little brother! Together, they graduated as junior accountants in June of 1944. Here, Renato talks about Giulio, his companion, during his last year in school:

At school, when he studied he was brilliant;
he learned Latin with great speed;
in accounting, he even was a giant,
a good candidate for the University.

We finished high school,
we graduated together as accountants
...The war burst out shattering the beautiful days,
which were lost in the darkness of black days ...

Here, Renato tells us about the war; of course, the experience of war occupies an important place in his DIARY:

The death squadrons ... the SS,
the tanks, the big bombings!
Dead people here, there ... serious wounds.
They filled up the sad moments with their screams.

Italy was full of Germans.
We learned and knew what was and is TERROR;
our country destroyed in half ...
no food on the tables,
religion disappeared, love vanished.

While Renato was under arms, paradoxically, it was Giulio who had the most dangerous adventure of the two. After earning his driver's license, he began working for his uncle Meneghetti's food company. Back then, this thriving business delivered food to the surrounding villages of Tuscany. The company gave Giulio a truck and it was his job to take the food from the warehouse and deliver it to Massarosa. During wartime, however, enemy aircrafts would strafe all means of transport; the truck Giulio was driving came under fire six times while delivering food. On those occasions, my father would escape through the passenger side door and run away from the road, huddling in a ditch or other safe place to avoid being hit by the bullets.

During one of his travels, Giulio met a Jewish family who asked him to help them reach Massarosa. Being a compassionate man, he felt pity and said he would assist them, despite the great risk. He hid the entire family behind food bags in the truck before beginning his journey toward Massarosa.

While he was on the road, a German patrol stopped him and pointed a tommy-gun at him, yelling and screaming in German that they would shoot if he didn't stop and ordering him to give them the keys of the truck. Giulio did not understand, but he did not panic. Remaining composed and responding with courtesy, he explained to the Germans that he would give them the truck, but before he could do that, he had to take his goods to Massarosa.

The Nazis wanted to see the goods. Giulio, with his heart pounding, prayed to the Lord that everything would be alright, and thanks to God, the soldiers saw only the food. The Jewish family was well hidden in the bottom of the truck.

The danger, however, was not over yet. As Giulio continued to explain how he would give them the truck when he was done with his delivery, two of the soldiers entered the passenger compartment with Giulio and said they were going to accompany him to Massarosa. They wanted to ensure they were going to receive the truck when he had finished delivering the food. And so, Giulio drove to Massarosa with two German soldiers sitting next to him.

When he arrived, my father distracted the soldiers with food and delicious local wine, so he could have time to unload the truck and allow the Jewish family to escape. It worked - the Germans didn't see the family exit the truck.

When Giulio was finished, he delivered the keys to the Germans, who took the truck and left. The Jewish family arrived unharmed and were tremendously grateful. My father had to walk all the way home that day, but he was thanking the Lord the whole way, for he had survived the hardest day yet of his life.

Giulio had every reason to be proud of himself: he had accomplished his duty by carrying the cargo to its destination, he had saved the lives of an entire Jewish family, and in the end ... he was back home and safe! His uncle Raimondo, however, was not appreciative. After Giulio told him the whole story about that incredible day, only one thing was clear to Raimondo: the company lost their truck. As a consequence, he decided that he was not going to pay Giulio, and forced him to work for a long time without pay.

Chapter 5
DURING THE WAR: HISTORICAL BACKGROUND FROM WAR TO NAZI EMPLOYMENT

On June 10th, 1940, from the balcony of Piazza Venezia in Rome, Benito Mussolini announced to an enthusiastic crowd that Italy would enter into the war alongside their German ally. He promised a short and victorious war. Instead, Italy wound up with thousands of dead or missing soldiers at the front, bombings of civilians, food rationing, and the drama of displaced citizens, who in one night had lost everything.

After the Anglo-American landing in Sicily on July 10th, 1943, King Vittorio Emanuele III decided to abandon and arrest Benito Mussolini, whom the Italians considered to be the main party responsible for the disasters.

Fascism had fallen, but the war was not over yet, for Italy was beginning one of the most traumatic periods of its history. Dino Grandi, a high-ranking official of Italy's fascist regime, and who contributed to the downfall of the dictator Benito Mussolini, was questioned by the sovereign.

Grandi warned him of the imminent danger the country was facing.
"If our army does not defend itself and does not counter the German invading forces already crossing the Brenner, and does not make any serious contact with the Allies, I expect terrible days for the nation."

During the famous radio broadcast on the evening of September 8th, 1943, the head of the Italian government, Marshal Badoglio, announced a secretly signed armistice between the Italian Kingdom and the Allied forces (United Kingdom and United States of America).

In the collective memory of the Italian people, this date is forever remembered as one of the most tragic moments of national history. "September 8" has become phrase that defines a chaotic situation, as well as material and moral corruption. In fact, the announcement of the armistice was followed by the sudden downfall of King Vittorio Emanuele III and Badoglio.

At dawn on September 9th, they departed from Rome and headed for Brindisi. Their officers remained, but without orders, the troops disbanded. Simultaneously, the Germans invaded northern-central Italy under the command of Marshal Albert Kesselring, but were obstructed by the first Italian partisan gangs.

THE GOTHIC LINE

The summer of 1944 brought northern Tuscany to the forefront of Italy's liberation war on Nazi occupation. In order to deal with the advancement of the Allies, the Germans built the so-called "Gothic Line" (*Gotenstellung*) on the Tosco-Emilian Apennine Mountains.

The Gothic Line was not a continuous line of fortifications, but a spattering of defenses that made use of the surrounding terrain: it crossed Italy from the Tyrrhenian coast to the north of Viareggio, all the way to the Adriatic Sea, reaching Pesaro. The line included thousands of camps, reinforced with concrete, wood, stone and with anti-tank ditches, barbed wire, and minefields surrounding them. Fortunately for the Allies, work on the Gothic Line was far behind schedule. At the time of the Anglo-American attack in September of 1944, construction of the Line in the Central Apennines was left behind, as the more vulnerable coasts needed to be fortified first. This left the Central Apennines open for the Allies to cross.

ANTI-PARTISAN OPERATIONS AND TERRORISM TOWARDS CIVILIANS.

In the summer of 1944, in the territory of the Apuan Mountains, the Italian rebel forces (called the Italian partisans) were numerous and sufficiently armed to assault the Germans with continuous attacks. They blew up bridges, attacked convoys, and killed soldiers, attempting to run the Germans out of their country.

For General von Zangen— the man responsible for building fortifications in the western sector of the Gothic Line— the danger presented by the partisans greatly disturbed construction of the defensive line; the partisans even caused a mass of workers to flee from the camps.

This intensification of the partisan guerrilla warfare and its successes resulted in an escalation of Nazi-fascist violence towards the civilian population. Citizens were accused of collaborating with the resistance, and for every German soldier killed by partisans, the Germans retaliated by killing ten Italian civilians.

They also displayed posters by the churches warning the population. In the minds of each German officer, this equation had now been formed: civilian = ally of the partisans. In June of 1944, Hitler himself gave orders to "reclaim" the areas near Nazi defensive lines. This reclamation meant eliminating partisan gangs and terrorizing populations suspected of supporting them. For the entire occupation forces, Hitler's directive was interpreted as free reign to torture civilians.

In the month that followed, the raids that commenced suggested a new phase of repression was beginning.

The Salani family from Viareggio was forced to move to Massaciuccoli, in the home of their maternal grandparents: Gesualda and Giulio Meneghetti. Renato and Giulio, realizing the danger they were experiencing with the massacres that took place in the surrounding towns, tried to find a safe place to live ... In the next chapter, you'll discover how they managed to survive.

The Nazis adopted macabre rituals to inflict terror and violence on the Italian population, including massacres in public squares, after which the corpses would be abandoned in the very place of execution, displaying and exposing the wounds.

In Filattiera (and its suburb of Ponticello), Lunigiana:

The cruel crime took place in Ponticello in the presence of all the population, men, women, children to whom, before the civilian execution, it was forbidden to cry by the German commander. On the same day in Filattiera, two civilians were hanged in the public square, of which the generalities could not yet be identified. These civilians were not recognized by the population: after the hanging they were beaten and sputtered.[1]

THE TERRIBLE SUMMER OF 1944

In view of the reclamation ordained by the Führer, evacuation measures were arranged for municipalities in central Italy. This evacuation of the Tuscan population was a punitive measure brought on by these words:

"The fights in the last few days have shown that the Italian male population provides significant aid to the enemy and, in part, actively contributes to the struggle against German troops."

The commander of the LXXV Army Corps, General Dostler, could not complete a total evacuation of the area between Massa and Carrara, so on July 31st, he delivered an order to General Simon (XVI SS-Panzergrenadier - Division-Reichsführer SS), in which he authorized him to shoot at anyone coming out of their house for the evacuation. His reasoning?

"In the first place, we cannot afford—in any case— to use particular regard. We must intervene inexorably."

The month of August inaugurated a new season of indiscriminate massacres in Versilia and Lunigiana, where General Simon operated his specialized anti-partisan unit.[1]

SANT'ANNA OF STAZZEMA: SLAUGHTER AT SUNRISE

In this violent climate, one of the most tragic episodes of the Italian Resistance occurred in a small village in the province of Lucca—the massacre of Sant'Anna di Stazzema, a small town in the mountains, 29 Km (18 miles) far from Massaciuccoli.

Sant'Anna di Stazzema was qualified by the German command as a "white zone"—a place to accommodate displaced persons. During the summer of 1944, the population outgrew the one thousand units provided for, and on July 26th, an evacuation order was issued. The German command distributed a press poster on the piazza of the Church of Sant'Anna, ordering all the inhabitants to leave their homes and move elsewhere.

Very few, however, obeyed this order. Entire families, with seniors and small children, would have had to walk through the Apennines, and face an uncertain future. They felt safer where they were and didn't want to move. According to some sources, the partisans also displayed a leaflet asking the people to stay firm and refuse the order.

Unfortunately, the town of Sant'Anna di Stazzema had been chosen for its exemplary military action. At dawn on August 12th, 1944, three units of Schutzstaffel (SS)—one of Hitler's major paramilitary organizations—climbed to Sant'Anna, while a fourth blocked each downhill route.

By seven o'clock the town was surrounded. When the SS and their guides arrived at Sant'Anna, the men of the town were gone. In hopes of avoiding being captured or deported, they had fled into the woods, leaving the women, children, and elderly to fend for themselves. The Germans entered the first homes of Sant'Anna and started dragging people from their homes. They locked the prisoners in stables, then turned and set fire to the houses. A survivor remembers:

"We were between 30 and 40 people, packed in a stifling heat. We spent an exhausting hour there and elderly people were fainting. Suddenly, a soldier opened the door and from the inside, we saw the outer light of a machine gun pointing toward us. After a few minutes of silence, we held our breath. Then the machine gun began to shoot in the thick midst of the prisoners. The bursts were repeated and the first rows were invested. It was a pandemonium, the end of the world. The first prisoners fell, I saw a German who continued to shoot and others throwing bombs. They also threw burning wood at us."[6]

This same scene was repeated several times in various other townships in the Sant'Anna area. In groups, the inhabitants were ruthlessly massacred with machine guns, rifles, and grenades. In stables, in alleyways, and in the squares—the Germans slaughtered them.

The tragedy came to a climax in the central plaza of the village, just in front of the church, where about 150 people—almost all women and children—were mutilated by machine guns. The corpses were crowded and burnt with flamethrowers.

By mid-morning, everything was over. The Germans left, leaving behind smoke rising from skeletons of buildings and carbonized bodies alike. In less than half a day, hundreds of civilians were killed, of whom only 350 could be identified. Among those victims, 65 were children under the age of ten. The youngest victim, Anna Pardini, was only 20 days old. Severely wounded, she was found screaming by her older sister, Cesira (she later received a gold medal for civil merit), who miraculously survived in the arms of her dead mother. Anna died a few days later in a hospital in Valdicastello.

As with so many other victims of Nazi atrocities, there was no justice for the dead in Sant'Anna di Stazzema, at least within a reasonable amount of time. Only in 2005, that is, 60 years later, La Spezia military tribunal sentenced the ten Nazi officers to imprisonment after finding them guilty of the war crimes in Sant'Anna. The soldiers were not held responsible; they had only carried out the orders of their superiors. The judgment was confirmed and finalized by the High Court in 2007.

Chapter 6
THE SALANI FAMILY DURING WAR TIME: FROM THE DISPLACEMENT TO IMPRISONMENT.

THE CAPTURE

Despite the war, Renato and Giulio graduated as junior accountants in June 1944. That same year, the evacuation orders reached them in Versilia. The whole Salani family was forced to move to Massaciuccoli and live in the country house of their Grandfather Giulio Meneghetti, as it was too dangerous to remain in the city of Viareggio.

The Salani family in front of Grandpa Giulio's house in Massaciuccoli before they were rounded up by the Germans. From the left: Ada, Euclide, Elsa, Maria, and Olga are standing. Giulio and Renato are squatting.

Entire towns were ransacked, and all men were taken as prisoners. Renato and Giulio avoided capture by hiding on a cargo boat that carried sand from the Massaciuccoli Lake to Viareggio. For days, the boat was their only home—they didn't dare leave it. Their sister Olga would sneak down to the boat to bring them food and water so they didn't starve.

Barcone: boat carrying sand from the Massaciuccoli Lake to Viareggio.[7]

The space below deck where Uncle Renato and dad slept had a tiled and tarred ceiling, and they noticed that a number "13" formed in the pattern of the tar. It was so distinct, one would have thought it had been put there on purpose. Although the number 13 is traditionally thought of as unlucky for some people, my uncle took it to be a sign of good luck—a sign that they would survive. He was right: it was indeed a number that turned out to be lucky for them.

While the brothers were staying in the boat, the rest of the family tried to live normally (as normal as could be in the middle of a war). Their monthly rations were becoming smaller and smaller: 180 grams of oil and butter and 150 grams of meat (including the bones) per month.

Those living in the countryside were more fortunate, as the roads to cities were impassable and means of communication had broken down (thanks to the Allies' bombings). Food and supplies were therefore hard to come by in the cities. This caused the already exorbitant prices of food on the black market to skyrocket: one flask of olive oil, £1100; one kilogram of sugar, £180; and workers—if they could even find work— only made £ 3 an hour. In June 1944, demonstrations were held in many villages of the Tuscan region calling for more food.

Despite all of these difficulties, steadfast Euclide did not give up his usual lifestyle and routine. He continued to teach music lessons, and enjoyed playing popular music on the piano for people on the streets to hear.
One day, some off-duty German soldiers walking in the streets heard Euclide's music as he was playing in his home.

The soldiers came in, and, seeing a cheerful environment, they started singing too. For several days, they continued coming back to listen to the music, to sing, and to have a good time. There were no more enemies—it was one of those charms that only MUSIC can create—no one was foreign, no one was an oppressor, no one was being oppressed. In that room, the Germans were no longer the cold executioners of homicidal orders, but merely men in the midst of a war, yearning for a taste of family and warmth that was so difficult to find away from home and were blessed by the momentary distraction that MUSIC brought to them.

Meanwhile, Renato and Giulio had left the boat and returned home, hoping the danger had already passed. Unfortunately ...

It was a turbid morning in mid-August
when early, suddenly, with loud noises
they showed up in our house, and in that moment
asked to gather all the men ...

Early that morning, before the sun had risen, Germans suddenly burst into their home, ransacking the place and rounding up all the Salani men. At 4 am on August 10th, 1944, Renato, Giulio, and Euclide were captured, with the exception of Grandpa Giulio, who was too elderly. My dad was sleeping in a small bed behind the main door, and when the soldiers opened it, they did not see him. Giulio could have safely escaped if he had remained still and quiet, but no: when he saw the Nazis seize his father and brother, he jumped up from his bed and exclaimed, "Wait, here I am! If you take them away, take me as well."

Uncle Renato, moved by Giulio's courage replied, "You didn't have to come with us! You didn't have to leave your bed, but since you are now a prisoner along with us, I assure and promise you that before Christmas, I'll take you back home healthy and safe!"

As they were ordered to walk towards Lucca, one of the German soldiers watching the column of prisoners recognized Euclide as the music teacher who had welcomed him into his home and had given him some moments of serenity. He waited until they had arrived a small village nearby, and whispered to Euclide, "Go. Go away. Go home."

On this occasion, it was MUSIC that saved my grandfather's life.

Music drives away hatred from those who are without love, gives peace to those who are in turmoil, it consoles those who are crying.
—Pablo Casals

TRAVELLING
When they were captured, Giulio was 19, Uncle Renato was 22, and both of them had just graduated as junior accountants.

They walked from Massaciuccoli to Lucca in columns of 10 to 15 men, and they were brought to a detention center called Casa Pia (once a nursing school, but by now the nuns were gone, as they had evacuated when the SS came). This place, once full of charity and hospitality, had been turned into a place devoid of warmth and full of hostility.

> *We were several men and well escorted*
> *by those cops who oh! How gloomy they were.*
> *Arriving, so deeply jaded,*
> *to Casa Pia, as hungry as wolves.*

All the prisoners were famished after walking for hours on end, from town to town, and yet they only received one loaf of bread per three prisoners. They were then kept locked up for two days, waiting for the trucks to take them to concentration camps. Hundreds of men were transported to the camps: 50 men on a truck, and three trucks at a time, they were carted away.

Here is Uncle Renato describing the landscape the prisoners saw from the truck while they were heading to the Fossoli Camp. They crossed the Porrettana and also passed by San Marcello Pistoiese.

*Beautiful alternating scenery,
the sad sight of villages
bombed by tremendous incursions
with ruined bridges ... and roads ... and roofs.*

They passed through Bologna, which had been reduced to rubble by bombs. However, despite the ruins, the streets were still animated with boys riding bikes and cars passing by. That brought such comfort to the prisoners, whose spirits were lifted when they saw that there was still life and the desire to live among the suffering and persecution.
The young prisoners kept their chins up and did everything they could to stay strong:

*We crossed the Dotta territory,
between a scream, a laugh and a joke.
It's our turn to thank Vittorio,
singing songs from Carnival of Viareggio.*

MUSIC had always accompanied Renato and Giulio, giving them strength and hope even in the most terrible of moments! Singing songs by Vittorio Tognarelli from the Carnival of Viareggio gave them and their fellow prisoners a bit of joy and desire to live, allowed them some moments to forget the fact that they were on their way to a concentration camp. While they still had the power to joke and sing, they still had some hope and autonomy, and it was easier to believe this nightmare soon would be over.

When they arrived in Bologna, Uncle Renato was able to write a postcard to his uncles and cousins, from San Martino Spino, Euclide's birthplace, warning them that they had been captured by the Germans and sent to the Fossoli concentration camp. When nightfall came, they continued on for Modena and the Fossoli Camp. Their spirits were still high, as these verses reveal:

... And listen to this ...
Among the women who came to talk with us,
I met Miss Arienti Raffaela,
who gave me a sense of personal satisfaction ...

*She's young and as gracious as anybody can see,
and she shows her kindness like I've never seen;
and she is from Bologna, just to say,
that if she captivates you, farewell,
you are in big trouble!*

Chapter 7
ARRIVAL AT FOSSOLI

We've arrived at the camp! Get out of the truck! Five men in line! Move!!!

I ruderi della chiesa del campo di concentramento di Fossoli.[7]

The Fossoli concentration camp was set up by the fascist regime in 1942 to confine prisoners of war—especially the British—captured in Africa. The camp changed its designation at the end of 1943, when (on the initiative of the Italian Social Republic) it became a place of internment of Jews and other political prisoners. This was in line with a directive issued in December of 1943 by Guido Buffarini, Minister of the Interior of the State created by Mussolini in Salò:

"This ordinance is for all the discriminated Jewish people, of any nationality and still residents in the country, they must be sent in special concentration camps. All their goods and properties must be subjected to immediate seizure waiting for confiscation. All those who were born from a Jewish marriage in application of the racial laws, and have gained recognition to belong to the Aryan race, must be subjected to special supervision by the police. In the meantime, Jewish convicts must be concentrated in provincial concentration camps waiting to be sent to special concentration camps specially equipped."

—Minister Buffarini

Shacks at Fossoli Concentration Camp.

Starting in February of 1944, the camp was managed directly by the Nazis. Its location—along the railway route leading to the Brenner—was considered particularly favorable by the Germans, as prisoners could be transferred easily from the Carpi-Fossoli station to the Reich lagers (an abbreviation of the German word for concentration camp, *konzentrationslager*) in Germany and Poland.

About five thousand political and racial prisoners interned in Fossoli were deported to tragic destinations, such as Auschwitz-Birkenau, Buchenwald, Bergen-Belsen, Mauthausen, and Ravensbruck. From January to August of 1944, of the eight railway convoys organized, five were destined for Auschwitz.

Fossoli: Departing train to Auschwitz.

The second of these convoys, with 650 deported prisoners, carried Primo Levi (an Italian Jewish chemist), who wrote about his brief stay at Fossoli in the beginning of his famous book *If this is a Man*, and in his poem *Sunset at Fossoli*.

A Jew and a partisan, Levi was arrested on December 13th, 1943, in Valle d'Aosta. He was sent to Fossoli and remained there until February of the following year, when he was deported to Auschwitz. He survived the lager and was able to return to Italy, where he devoted himself to recording the atrocities he saw and suffered through. He wanted to ensure the memory of those horrific experiences was never lost—that the world may be ever vigilant and never let those barbaric practices happen again. Primo Levi also deserves merit for highlighting the uniqueness of the *Shoah* (the Hebrew term for the extermination of the Jews) in the history of humanity. Anti-Semitism has unfortunately always existed, and in history there are countless episodes of persecution of Jews, but before 1942, no one had planned—so methodically and scientifically—to erase an entire community from the face of the Earth.

Never before had a state organized such a vast and ruthlessly efficient concentration apparatus, where death only came after an unnumbered series of physical and emotional tortures, inflicted with the purpose of eradicating any residue of human dignity in the individual. "The hell of a madman" is what the camps of extermination were called by one survivor. They were places where the rules were constantly changing, which made it all the more terrifying—their unpredictability kept everyone on edge.

Primo Levi's book *If this is a Man*[2] is well-known, but his lesser-known poem *Sunset at Fossoli* (written in 1946 and subsequently published in the book *At Uncertain Time*[3]), in my opinion, deserves to be read by wide audiences. For this reason, I'd like to share it here:

Sunset at Fossoli

I know what it means to never go back

Across the barbed wire

I saw the sun go down and die;

I felt my lacerated flesh

The words of the old poet:

"They can only fall and go back:

To us, when the short light is off,

An endless night is to be slept.[3]

The shacks of a Nazi Concentration Camp surrounded by barbed wire networks.

In 1944, the Fossoli camp was placed under the direction of the office of the General Directorate for the Occupation of Labor in Germany. Thus, in addition to Jews and political prisoners, the camp began to house men and women captured by the Germans to be used for cooperative work in the territories of the Third Reich. It was at this time (and for this reason) that the Salani brothers were interned in the Fossoli camp, since they were not Jews and had not been involved in any political activities.

Chapter 8

TESTIMONIALS OF THE SURVIVORS

In this chapter, you will read testimonials from survivors. You may be wondering, though, why I included these, and what they have to do with the story of the Salani brothers. The answer is simple: I am writing this to the younger generations, so that they can learn the history of World War II and never forget. Only knowing and remembering the mistakes of the past we can hope that humanity will reflect on these and never repeat them again. I refer in particular to the *Shoah*, the racial laws, the persecution of Jewish citizens, the Italians who were deported from their own homes, and the imprisonment and death of many civilians. I am hoping to honor those who, although in different fields and deployments, opposed the project of extermination at the risk of their own lives, and saved and protected the persecuted.

1) FOSSOLI CAMP IN 1942.

Originally, Fossoli camp was destined for prisoners of war. In fact, in the summer of 1942, when the largest advance of the German army was in European territory, many prisoners were brought and forced to labor in the Fossoli concentration camp. There were over 3,000 inmates—mostly soldiers and under-officers of the Allied forces, including British, South African, Australian and New Zealanders. They arrived in echelons, walking all the way from Carpi station to the concentration camp, arousing sorrow and compassion from the villagers who saw them walking towards the camp.

At that time, the Fossoli camp was directed and administered by the Command of the Royal Italian Army and was subject to the International Hague Convention. The life of the prisoners was generally acceptable: detainees had their own internal organization, they worked, and they received a modest wage. Here is the testimony of a British prisoner:

"We regularly received the Red Cross parcels, the food was pretty good in the camp, and most of the prisoners kept fit very well by playing football or boxing! I also practiced these sports. With the few Lire we received every week, we could buy what was needed for our personal cleaning and also the tomatoes that the Italians brought to the store inside our camp. All of them also gave a few bucks to buy musical instruments to form a small orchestra. Sometimes the guards allowed us to buy melons in a farmhouse. The Italian linen cleaner came every week to get dirty clothing to return them clean. We became friends, as I learned a bit of Italian and he brought me, along with some eggs, Italian newspapers that our camp journalists translated for us and put into the news bulletin board."

—Alfred Moore.

2) FOSSOLI CONCENTRATION CAMP IN 1944

As I mentioned earlier, in 1944 the Fossoli camp was transferred to the German administration and became a sorting camp for prisoners who labored while waiting to be deported to a German or Polish lager. Consequently, the prisoners' living conditions were very different from those described by the British officer.

"At the entrance, some cabins were used as offices and accommodations for the SS guards of the Camp that was surrounded by a spiked metal mesh. The towers on which the sentinels were located were beyond the net. One side of the camp was a few meters from the road were transit was permitted, but on the edge of the road, giant signs warned: "Dangerous area, shooting without warning." At the entrance of the camp, a huge black flag was raised day and night."

—Enea Fergnani[4]

Barbed wire fences that surrounded the Fossoli Camp. Behind are the shacks for Jewish families and political opponents.

The sighting tower, positioned beyond the barbed wire net, from which the SS sentinels were watching the prisoners.

3) ARRIVAL CEREMONIES

"They cut our hair to nothing with a razor. We picked the straw mattresses, a blanket, the lunchboxes, and glasses; we went through a brief medical visit. They left us several hours with only shoes, waiting for our clothes and our linen to be disinfected by the autoclave, and in the meantime, they made us take a shower.

Then, they sent us to the office of the command to defer our generalities and receive the new serial number. Then the head of the camp arrived to give us his instructions: we cleaned the cabin and placed the straw mattresses on the floor and received the new cabinet instructions, an endless forced commitment...

In the evenings, we were able to take part to the prisoners' roster where Germans would call our names. This didn't happen. Men were not considered as such, and it's not true that men could use their words and say, 'present'. Here, nobody is called, and no one needs to answer "here", because interns are considered as numbers, so there is no need to call their names... They just count the numbers."

—Don Paolo Liggeri[4]

4) REGISTRATION

"I was subjected to the torture of enrollment. It was necessary to declare our own generalities many times: they were always written in Italian and German, so every time hard-working translations had to be done.

Then we had to take face and profile photos, fingerprints, and do collective washing. They shaved us to nothing, they wanted the disinfestation of our personal garments in the autoclave, then they gave us a greenish-gray military shirt and two long white linen panties (those with the cords at the bottom).

On both of these garments our number and a red triangle was applied. Jewish prisoners had a yellow rectangle; foreign convicts had a blue rectangle."

—Arrigo Boccolari

5) THE SMELL OF FOSSOLI CAMP

"My companions and I took possession of an empty cabin: number 17/A. The bunk beds made of poplar, and the fetid and used straw mattresses and blankets all emanated a nauseating smoky smell. The air of Fossoli was impregnated with the smell of bed bugs being cooked in an autoclave. From that kiln came out a steady and sweet smoke. As long as I write, I feel—after sixteen years—those stings that scratch my throat."

—Arrigo Boccolari[4]

6) HUNGER

"Those like me who don't have any kind of relief or help from outside, are always hungry.

Maybe because the food is scarce (black broth in the morning, a small bread and two unseasoned soups), or maybe because moving from the mephitic air of the cell where we slept to the open air of the camps that surrounded us, awakened our appetites. Hunger is so fond of us that it gives us stomach cramps. Luckily, in the camp, they set up a small grocery store that sells the most disparate foods (according to the choices of the day and only one type of food per day). The assignment for our cabin is so scarce that we can easily distribute a small square piece of chestnut cake or a spoonful of ricotta cheese per person. Today, however, it is getting better, because a free cash fund was set up for comrades without money and the dispensary gave us a large amount of today's commodity. Too bad they were onions. Only onions—a small mountain of onions."

—Don Paolo Liggeri

7) GETTING ORGANIZED

"We have to start organizing. The soup is poor and terrible, bread is scarce, and we are missing almost all the indispensable tools of civil life.

We made arrangements with the chef and established that we had to provide a fund for distributing to everyone—even those who couldn't afford to pay—a more nutritious and abundant soup. Another fund will be used for purchasing other groceries: fruit, ricotta cheese, and eggs. Even these can be distributed free of charge to those who have no money. Dr Befana and Dr. Sforzini compile the list of most commonly used medicines. Others compile lists of various items to buy in Carpi: razors, soap, letter paper, nibs for pens, shoe polish, combs, brushes, and mirrors. Several companions of goodwill offer us their services and some already wash and mend or sew up our linen. Since we are allowed to write a letter or postcard every fifteen days and receive parcels, we will have everything we need in a couple of weeks."

—Enea Fergnani

8) A SHOOTING

"The other prisoners were beginning to stand in line to be controlled, and shortly thereafter, I joined them. The German marshal Ricoff started calling numbers.

They were the interns who, on that day, had to work on the shift. Wait! A gunshot, and one of the workers thudded to the ground. He was a deaf and mute man who had not obeyed the order immediately. He was slow answering to the roster. The other workers kept silent. 'He died,' said our Jewish doctor, De Benedetti. Silently, everyone left; there was only that immobile body on the ground."

—Alba Valech Capozzi,

(One of the Jewish women prisoners in the Fossoli camp)

9) FAMILIES

"Every evening, for about an hour, the Germans opened the gate of the men's camp and many families could meet, although it was for a short time."

—Alba Valech Capozzi [4]

10) DEPARTURE

"With absurd accuracy, we later had to become accustomed to the list that the Germans gave to the prisoners. At the end, the marshal asked: 'Wieviel stück?' (How many pieces?) and the corporal greeted excitedly, and replied that the "pieces" were six hundred and fifty, and that everything was in order.

Then they loaded us into the wagons and they brought us to the Carpi station, where the train and the escorts were waiting for us for the journey…

Here we received the first shots and punches; this event was so new and senseless that I did not feel any pain in either my body or soul. Just a deep astonishment: how can one man hit another man without anger and without a reason? The wagons were twelve and we were six hundred and fifty. In my wagon, there were only forty-five people, but it was a small wagon."

—Primo Levi[2]

11) PRAYERS

"The priests who were interned at Fossoli with me were nine, and they all secretly carried out our ministry. My shack—which was earlier N. 16th and later N. 20th—in the evening, turned into a chapel.

There was a team of young men from Vicenza, 100% Catholics, who were my faithful followers. One of them was the guard, to warn us when the SS approached and we recited the Rosary in the most hidden corner in a soft voice and sang the litanies of Our Virgin Mary.

Outside, in the plaza of the camp, the interns were having a good time: someone played music, others danced and laughed. These spring mountains were so sweet and beautiful! The sun sank slowly into a sea of fire at the extreme limits of a boundless plain. The suavity and gentleness of that time invoked happiness. The music and the accordion sound came to us, but it did not affect our meditation. In contact with God, we felt stronger and more serene than those who were looking for comforting the afflictions of the day with some music or in two turns of waltz."

—Don Sante Bartolai[4]

These remembrances No. 11 and 12 testify the fact that the Salani brothers were playing MUSIC with the accordion, singing, dancing and entertaining the prisoners of the camp during their recreation hour, bringing them a little happiness and desire of living after their daily sufferings.

12) LEISURE

"The shacks of Jewish men and women were surrounded by a barbed wire, and during the day it was forbidden to communicate with other prisoners. In the evening, after the meal, seclusion ceased and then the camp's square assumed the appearance of a swarming village on a holiday. Walking far and wide, couples in all directions, accordion tunes and some dancing too—why not? After all, life had to be taken as it came, and they needed to enjoy the pleasant company of women as much as they could."

—Don Paolo Liggeri[4]

13) FURIO GABBRIELLI

Furio Gabbrielli was a brotherly friend of the Salani brothers, who was deported to Germany and interned at a concentration camp with his father. Here are his memories.

"God really helped me, oh God! Trying to keep away those past days, when memories return, it maims my brain and psyche."

Furio and his father were caught by the Germans in Massarosa (a province of Lucca) and shipped immediately to Kahla, in the woods of Thuringia, to a German lager.

"We were raked in Massarosa in August 1944, with a few clothes. I was 17 years old and I saw my father dying of hunger on a straw mattress full of bedbugs in the lager cabin. Beside him, others who were dying of hunger, whose skeletons were swollen with nephrites. I had to leave him in the cabin every morning and go to work on Walpersberg Hill, without knowing if I would find him alive in the evening. Peak and shovel for ten hours, rain, wind, and snow. I was still standing even though I weighed thirty-nine kilograms (85 Pounds) on the weight scale of the Grosseutersdorf Camp infirmary. In November, the cold became intense; they gave us gloves and long undergarments, but many of us began to get sick. Those who were sick and remained in the camp could only eat halb portion (half-portion) of food. They wrote on the walls of the shacks in many languages: "Those who do not work, do not eat." When one of us fell exhausted on the floor, we would soon get beaten with a wooden stick.

One morning, my team was sent to Kahla Railway Station to unload iron bars from the wagons and reload them onto trucks. Ten hours of this job without eating under a cold drizzle in December. In the evening, when we crossed Kahla, returning to the lager, I missed my strength and fell short of breath. I leaned on a wooden fence by the cemetery—I do not know how many minutes. My companions abandoned me, they were too hungry to care for me. Suddenly, a man and a woman came up in front of me; she was taller and had a large amount of white hair. There was some moonlight, so I could see they were looking at me. They approached me, to see me better. 'Oh ... so jung' ... (oh, so young) she said. Her voice was full of pity. 'Wie alt bis du?' (How old are you?) She asked. Siebzehn (seventeen), I answered. It seemed like a miracle. It was the first time I saw Germans feel pity. I answered everything, I said who I was, that my companions had abandoned me, that I was going back to the camp to wait for the soup, and my father was expecting me...if he was still alive. The white-haired lady told me then that her name was Bechmann, that she lived at Rollestrasse 15, and that she wanted to give me some food. 'Bitte komme. Vergiss nicht' (come, do not forget. Even tomorrow...) Her husband nodded.

This German family, noble of feelings, risked their lives to save me. They were helped out by five trusted friends and acquaintances, who acted in utmost secrecy in order not to be punished or killed by the Nazis. Seven human beings who kept the courage to remain humans at a time when Germans were asked to be inhumane. My judgment on all Germans has always been conditioned by these seven people.

On January 10, my father could not survive to the stents and malnutrition, and unfortunately died.

It is from that day in 1945 that I strive to keep away that past. To alleviate the trauma. To stay normal. By now I'm seventy, I've almost succeeded ... God gave me a hand."

—Furio Gabbrielli.[5]

Chapter 9

LIFE IN THE FOSSOLI CONCENTRATION CAMP

FIRST DAY AT THE CAMP

*Oh God! What a strange effect it has caused,
in our hearts that strong light!
Everyone had become accustomed to the dark.
What a spontaneous exclamation we made.*

*Through a barbed-wire gate,
we went into the camp to sleep,
and inside a big and illuminated bedroom,
they left us alone without saying one word.*

After traveling for hours in the truck, all the prisoners—now used to the darkness of night—were blinded by the dazzling lights as they rode into camp. They passed through a barbed-wire gate and entered the field. The Germans took them to a bedroom with other detainees, who, upon their arrival, overwhelmed them with all kinds of questions.

A lot of people came to us asking
when we were taken, where we came from;
they were from all over, and as we spoke,
it was announced that we were leaving soon.

But I was tired from the long journey
so, I lay on my bed to rest,
enveloped by the noise of my fellow prisoners
those riders, those knights, I understood them.

When they were assigned their bunk bed, they prepared their mattresses and Renato noticed their bunk bed's number: 26 (= 13 + 13)! This detail made him very happy, and he was once again convinced that number 13 was a sign of good luck. He immediately turned to Giulio with words of comfort, "You will see, we will get out of here soon!"

Bunk beds at Fossoli Camp.

Soon, the insects came to meet the newcomers:

A huge army of bugs attacked us:
They came to me
while I lay thinking;
flies, bugs, fleas, and some more,
insects that I had never seen before.

*I jumped like them; I did the same,
trying to defend myself, beating the air:
slapping, hitting – I was obsessed!
Those disgusting creatures only good for sucking blood.*

*We jumped out of bed and scratched
 all over until two am.
I said, "Oh, if only we could leave…"
Our eyes were wide like oxen.*

*You'll see that we will get lucky,
thanks to the No.13 on our bunk beds,
I said; we happened to be sent here by chance,
we will have no bad luck; Giulio, you will see.*

No. 13 STARTS BRINGING GOOD LUCK

The next morning, Uncle Renato picked up his soap and towel and was heading to the bathroom when a German officer came inside the cabin and asked, "Who among you knows how to use a typewriter? Raise your hand."

Uncle Renato wanted to go take a shower and had no intention of presenting himself or responding to the officer's request, but my father begged him to raise his hand to see where the request might lead. Reluctantly, Renato raised his hand and the officer told him to follow him, and so he did. After an interview and a test of his typewriting skills, he was immediately put to work by the German soldiers.

With his background in accounting and his previous secretarial duties to the navy commander, Renato had become an excellent typist. The Germans said they would postpone his departure for Germany, and while Uncle Renato was happy at this prospect, he could not abandon Giulio to his fate. He told the soldiers that he had a brother among the prisoners who was also an accountant, and said that if they accepted him to work in the office too, he would remain alongside him. Otherwise, Renato would go to Germany with Giulio.

Thank God, they took on Giulio and tasked him with putting the carbon copy between the sheets of paper Renato had to fill out. Giulio typed as well, helping to finish the documents faster. A German officer would then check their work. They were actually paid £1,000 a month for this job as concentration labor camp workers.

The documents Renato and Giulio had to type were contracts that categorized all the prisoners in the camp by number. Those whose numbers were under contract No. 1 were dispatched to Germany, those with No. 2 stayed in Italy to work for the Germans, and No. 3 was assigned to seriously ill people (suffering from tuberculosis, for example), to let them go and die with their families and not spread disease amongst the German soldiers.

These documents were also labor contracts, but they were not the typical kind of labor contracts—the labor was being forced on the workers, and if they disobeyed or tried to escape, they were shot.

Here, Uncle Renato describes the scene when the Germans asked for a typist:

I was on my way to the bathroom,
When, annoyingly, my destiny changed.
Giulio said, "Go, you'll go to the bathroom later,
write for them from A to Zed first."

They took me to a very modest office
consisting of a medium-tall closet,
three typewriters, two stoves and a cabinet
that works as a room divider, enough to condemn.

So, I'm confirmed in the office,
and I was working passionately,
but Giulio is about to be visited by the camp's doctor,
therefore, I have to make the right decision.

Quickly, I approach Mr. Holzer,
tell him that Giulio is also an accountant.
"If he remains I am happy;
if not, I'll go with him - I will not stay."

But Mr. Holzer agreed, and
Giulio was also hired,
applying the carbon copy paper,
doing his work very diligently.

The joy in both our hearts
(as we were not going to be dispatched)
found the limited border of the camp,
and to see Giulio look out beyond the fences,
satisfied me so much.

THEIR FRIENDS DISAPPEARED. OSVALDO

Even though the brothers were joyful of escaping the dangers of a Nazi lager by finding a job, sadness crept in again, as they saw so many of their dear friends depart. They cultivated, in their hearts, the hope of embracing them again, soon—when they would meet again at home.

But after a few hours,
our hearts are filled with melancholy:
Yes, our friends are leaving, what a torment;
our friends are sent away ...

I kiss and embrace them all, one by one
and I pretend not to feel anything,
one joke to one, one word to another,
while inside I worry atrociously!

So long Nino, Mauro, Antonio ... Bye Carlo;
Goodbye - I'll see you soon back home:
If there is any danger, be ready to avoid it,
and everywhere you go, try to display the best side
of Viareggio ...

This way our friends left,
and after them many others too were gone.
If, however, we were happy for our destiny,
We pitied the other rounded up friends...

Unfortunately, their dear friends never returned ...

Years ago, Giulio told my brother Leonardo the very sad story of Osvaldo, a close friend and neighbor from Viareggio, who was raided by the German guards the same day as they were, and transported with them to the Fossoli concentration camp. Osvaldo's family was very good to the Salani family and often sent fresh vegetables to them from their garden when food became scarce.

Osvaldo was a young man with thick red hair and a rebellious nature. In the camp he was stubborn and did not bend easily to what the guards commanded; he began plotting a revolt among the prisoners. Unfortunately, the Germans caught on, and, to set an example, they hanged him with barbed wire in front of the rest of the prisoners.

Giulio and Renato were working in the administrative office when they heard the news of the horrific death of their friend, and they became utterly distraught. Osvaldo's gruesome death sent shock waves through the whole camp, and when news of his death eventually reached his family and friends in Viareggio, they were horrified.

NEW AND OLD FRIENDS

After working for several months in the administration office at Fossoli, my father met a girl named Elvea. She was very friendly, sensitive, and serious—a cute girl who inspired confidence. Elvea was from Modena and was employed by the SS to work in the office together with two other girls, sisters Bruna and Maria.

Giulio and Renato were tasked with teaching the three girls to use the typewriter, as the Germans wanted to employ them and send the Salani brothers to the German lagers. However, the girls were fond of the Salani brothers, so they wasted time and pretended they were not able to type. Thus, they managed to avoid, or at least delay, Giulio and Renato's deportation to Germany.

In the picture above, you can see the office of the Fossoli Camp with the three typewriters where Giulio and Renato worked. Giulio standing between Elvea and Maria as he shows them how to draft the contracts of the concentration camp. Behind is Renato next to Bruna. All this under the close supervision of a German officer. This photo was taken by Dr. Nesi, a physician at Fossoli Camp. Behind the photo, the date: 16/11/1944.

This is none other than Furini Elvea,
when she wears white, oh how cute she is!
She looks like a rose, but a tea rose,
or a butterfly that lies on the flowers ...

I wonder if Giulio would like to have a family,
with that amethyst-eyed young girl.
... Elvea came in with a new company
with that little girl, do you know, Maria?
with whom Nesi photographed us.

Yes, because... wait! ... I have to explain:
Elvea wanted to have Giulio near her,
so he would be by her side in the picture,
and she would keep the photo by her heart.

Well! Finally, the day was beautiful,
the sun darted with heat;
and for Giulio, who had worn a tie,
it was impossible to have her away from his heart.

Thanks to the office work they had been given, Renato and Giulio were privileged: they could continue to wear their clothes instead of the uniforms the other prisoners had to wear. It may seem like a small thing, but I think it had great psychological value. That clothing was a thread that still tied them to their "normal" lives. It was a small, thin bridge to the future—a quick return to home and the normality of life in peace.

Photo from left to right: Giulio, Elvea, Renato, Bruna, and a friend of theirs—a fellow prisoner who worked in the camp.

Every now and then, they received a special permit to leave the camp under strict rules. So, on a Sunday, Renato, Giulio, and Elvea went to Mass in Carpi.

We wanted to go to Carpi,
that misty, foggy and drizzling day.
We wanted to go to Mass,
in the Duomo with radiant Elvea.

In the afternoon, what a coincidence,
we went for a coffee
and there was great pleasure
in finding a piano at Bar Milano.

Oh! what a joy, to touch the keyboard!
That keyboard like a mouth of black and white teeth!
Here is a ninth chord played my way...
I started playing, stopping only when I was tired.

I played and improvised... And I went on playing songs that reminded me of something:
Both beautiful and ugly tunes, serenades,
one after the other without pausing.

Local lady, lovely lady,
I still remember your great heart;
You are kind ... and then, I repeat beautiful!
for you I'll still play ... here! A nice chord.

Here is Renato on a bicycle on November 16th, 1944.

Renato with Elvea (left) and Bruna (right).

One day, Nullo Viti, a dear friend and schoolmate of the brothers who graduated as junior accountant with them back in Viareggio, arrived at Fossoli Camp. Giulio and Renato saved Nullo's life by advising him to avoid showing up for his medical exam, knowing it would lead to a clean bill of health and therefore to No. 1 contract.

Being in the administrative office, they secretly assigned him a No. 2 contract, thus avoiding deportation to one of the Nazi lagers and risking their lives by doing so. Nullo was sent to work in the grocery store, near the kitchen. In a short time, he became a friend of the cook and her husband, and—thanks to them—at last Renato and Giulio's access to food began to improve. They enjoyed various local dishes, including risottos (risotto is a rice dish with vegetables, mushrooms or meat sauce).

We ate pasta and cappelletti,
legumes soup or very good broth.
Yet it was Mrs. Aletti
who, very nicely, wanted to serve us her way.

We had white and good bread in large quantities,
and for cigarettes ... hmm ... I do not complain
We were four good friends ...

How exquisite were those cappelletti,
with broth made by fifteen chickens.
And the wine? And the apples, and the other items,
that were there and were so sweet?

To tell you the truth we cannot complain.
Why, what do you mean? We're doing relatively well,
since we are able to settle down,
sleeping all four into a room.

For one hour each evening, the Germans would open the gates separating the men's and women's camps, and husbands and wives could finally unite and embrace. During that recreational time, Uncle Renato played the accordion, while Giulio sang. All the prisoners danced and had fun, forgetting their sorrows for a moment. Again, MUSIC was essential in keeping morale high, inspiring hopes for the future.

> "Music is the shorthand of emotion"
> (Leo Tolstoy).

And then we danced every night,
our bodies giving off sparks.
At last we had fun, do you want to know why?
They told us: Here you are,
for you, one thousand Liras.

THE MYSTERY OF THE TYPEWRITTEN TOILET PAPER

Finally, the time has come to reveal to you why Uncle Renato's DIARY was typed on TOILET PAPER...

The typewriter the brothers worked on was readily available to them, given the job they had been entrusted with, however, the only paper they could use for free was the toilet paper from the camp.

Considering the deprivations, hunger, and suffering of all prisoners in the camp, finding TOILET PAPER was a real luxury, but the real mystery is how these scrolls kept for more than 70 years, with the writing Renato had imprinted on them sharply.

The fact is, TOILET PAPER then was not like the plush, cottony, soft, layered material we use today: it was a robust and durable paper, pungent and scratchy, too! This, and the great care Aunt Alma took of the paper, is why the unorthodox DIARY is still in good condition. In fact, I believe the love and devotion Alma has for this and other precious documents is the real secret of its perfect preservation.

Chapter 10
NULLO VITI

Nullo's interview (June 23rd, 2016)

Nullo Viti was Renato and Giulio's classmate, who graduated with them at the Istituto Superiore di Istruzione Carlo Piaggia in Viareggio, and has always been a great, fraternal friend of the Salanis. For this reason, I wanted to dedicate an entire chapter to his story of the war, which is interwoven with Renato and Giulio's.

ORGANISATION TODT

The Organisation Todt (OT) was founded in Germany in the 1930s, by engineer Fritz Todt, as an infrastructure company dedicated to developing innovative techniques for that era. With the outbreak of the Second World War, its activity extended to all the countries occupied by Germany, becoming an essential support to the war effort.

Todt was tasked with the construction of military installations of various kinds, the repair of damage caused by enemy bombings, and the strengthening of industries useful for war purposes. In Italy, Todt was involved, inter alia, with the construction of the Gothic Line. It was a paramilitary organization, whose senior officials were senior citizens. During the war, the OT exploited millions of men for work (namely military and civilians recruited forcibly), but there were also volunteers—Nullo Viti was one. In fact, he had been called to the army, but he did not show. He was hired by the OT to avoid being indicted as a draft dodger.

At first, Nullo worked in the minefields in Massa and Carrara. One of his companions was hit by an anti-man mine explosion (less catastrophic than an anti-tank mine, but still deadly). That man lost a leg and died, not immediately, but after a great deal of suffering.

The organization's treatment of workers was certainly not enviable. Meals consisted of *sbroscia* (pig swill), dried cabbage, and grass, which emanated a nauseating odor. After working hard all day in deadly fields, that disgusting slop was a really underwhelming meal, to say the least ... One day in Carrara, Nullo was fortunate enough to buy a loaf of bread, which he nibbled on in order to make it last longer.

The disciplinary system in the OT was similar to that of the concentration camps. In Sarzana, one of the workers who had tried to escape was arrested and shot on the spot. Nullo was ordered to dig the pit and bury him, but he went into hiding to avoid the gruesome task. Two brothers tried to escape on the way to Pontremoli, but they were also captured and killed.

On a summer night in 1944, Nullo and his companions were brought to the Fossoli concentration camp. He felt the same sensations and lived through the same experiences as the Salani brothers, who had come to Fossoli just shortly before: the blinding glow of the night lighting, the assignment to a bunk bed, and the sleepless nights while facing the assaults of bedbugs and fleas.

The next morning, just outside of the dormitory, Nullo saw in the distance, beyond the barbed wire fence, a familiar face: it was Giulio.

He called out to him, "Oh, Giulio! ... But... What are you doing here?"

My father replied, "What am I doing? They took me before you. Renato is here, too. Wait, what are *You* doing here?!"

Again, Giulio and Renato saved Nullo's life by advising him not to take his medical exam, knowing it would lead to a clean bill of health and therefore deportation to a German lager." Renato and Giulio managed to secure a N. 2 contract for Nullo, and keep him working at the camp in the grocery store.

From the left: Nullo Viti, Bruna, Elvea, and Giulio. Photo taken by Dr. Nesi at the Fossoli Camp on November 16th, 1944.

Then, on November 29th, 1944, the Fossoli camp was bombed, and though he had a chance to escape, Nullo decided to remain in order to avoid greater uncertainties of being captured outside and possibly getting killed. Renato and Giulio chose a different path - and their fate and the perilous adventure which followed will be revealed in Chapter 11.
 Aside from trying to avoid danger,

133

Nullo's choice to stay was based on the fact that also he didn't want to lose his job at the grocery store, which was actually quite profitable. The bombing, however, had made the camp uninhabitable, so the detainees were transferred to the concentration camp of Gonzaga in the Mantova area.

Nullo continued to work for the Germans even at Gonzaga; this time in the office. He became a very dear friend of Dr. Nesi, the camp physician, and together they made a pact: if they survived, they would make a pilgrimage by foot to the shrine of Our Lady of the Guard in Bologna.

After the war, they kept their promise.

On December 30th, 1944, three hundred partisans attacked the Gonzaga camp. They captured and shot the Germans in that camp, including thirty-four senior officers of the OT. Only two survived, feigning death under the bodies of their comrades who shielded them from the bullets.

On April 25th, 1945, the day of liberation, the war finally ended. Nullo saw American trucks and tanks parading day and night. For 48 hours, a continuous stream of vehicles traveled through Bondeno, crossing the River Po.

Nullo pedaled to Bologna on the bicycle he had bought with money earned from working in the camp. From there, he got on a truck and passed through Pistoia, Lucca, and on May 1st, 1945, he finally arrived at Seravezza, where he found his mother. In tears of joy, they embraced. His mother told him she received news of him from the Salani brothers when they arrived in Massaciuccoli, after escaping from Fossoli.

They went to see her, and assured her that her son was doing well, that he had found a job in the grocery store of the concentration camp, and that he was not lacking anything. Renato and Giulio were disappointed, though, that Nullo had decided to remain in Fossoli to continue his job.

To this day, Nullo is still immensely grateful to Giulio and Renato, who saved him from deportation (and likely death) by giving him the precious "contract No. 2."

"The Salanis have remained for me dear friends! Friendships like the Salanis, I had really very few! "

The relationship between Nullo and the Salani brothers was a one of not only gratitude, respect, and admiration, but also fun, thanks to the MUSIC that has always been a part of their lives—keeping their spirits lifted in times of trial.

Several years after the war, Nullo, Renato, and Giulio shared other experiences of intense emotion, such as their pledged visit the sanctuary of Our Lady of Medjugorje. Nullo still remembers the evenings at the hotel, when Uncle Renato played the piano, and my dad sang alongside with Alma and Nancy (my aunt and my mom). The guests and employees all enjoyed listening to them.

Years later, Nullo went to visit the Salanis in Venezuela (where they had moved), and often recalls the many adventures they had together: all those adventures, beautiful and ugly, had contributed to a deep friendship and deeper affection—one which lasts for a lifetime.

In this late 1970's photo, Nullo is the first on the left, with my brother Sergio. Lino Ceragioli (center) and Giulio Salani (right) at the Macuto Sheraton hotel in Venezuela.

Chapter 11
KISSED BY FORTUNE

AN UNEXPECTED VISIT

One day at the camp, Giulio and Renato received an unexpected and welcome visit from some relatives who lived in San Martino Spino, near Modena. They had finally received the letter from Renato saying that they were being detained at the Fossoli concentration camp, so they rushed to visit them, thinking they were suffering greatly. In Modena, the population was still very lively and generous, so Aunt Sara, Uncle Gino, and their sons Adriano and Laura, brought them gifts, warm hugs, and, above all, joy, which inspired Renato to use one of Dante's quotes from the sonnet of the Divine Comedy "*So Kind and Honest She Seems*".

The joy of seeing them was so great
"Which cannot be understood by those who
feel it not."
They brought gifts for both of us,

a pair of underpants, some bread, a chicken and a new t-shirt ....

Their relatives said they would come back to visit them again, but seeing that they were not doing as terribly as they had imagined, they never came back.

*They told us that another time again
they would be back to visit us;
but we haven't seen them so far,
and we cannot leave the camp!!!*

*This way I passed my days and life inside the camp,
privileged by fortune.
The days are as fast as a flash,
and we sing to the sky and to the moon.*

*We spent one month
with Bruna and her sister;
The first woman, already good-natured,
with her big, plump lips and upturned nose...*

BRUNA'S COURAGE

Bruna was one of the three girls who worked in the office with Giulio and Renato, and she was the main person responsible for arranging the escape of my father, my uncle, and other prisoners in the camp.

She became the friend, lover, and mistress of German commander Zimmerman, but did not do so for either love or personal gain: her purpose was to provide information to her brother, a partisan leader who commanded an active brigade in the mountains near Bologna.

The information gathered by Bruna was valuable in organizing resistance and fighting the Germans.

Working with them in the office, Bruna grew fond of Giulio and Renato and decided to help them. To fulfill her plan, she needed to wait for a night when Commander Zimmerman was sleeping deeply. When that night came, she gathered all her courage, got out of bed and took his jacket from the armchair where it was hung, trying desperately to control her shaking hands and trembling fingers. She rummaged around in the pockets and finally found what she was looking for: the commander's heat stamp, the small object that could decree life, death, liberty, or deportation.

Earlier, Giulio and Renato had drafted two permits on their behalf, claiming they were suffering from tuberculosis and, as such, could be allowed to leave the camp. However, these documents meant nothing without Zimmerman's stamp—the stamp now in the hands of their friend Bruna. She stamped both documents and, shaking from fear, put the stamp back in Zimmerman's jacket pocket and went back to bed.

I've never met Bruna, and my father has not heard any news of her since they escaped; I do not know if she is dead or alive. For me, though, she has always been a reference point, an example to inspire me, and a character to reflect on. I understand the importance that—in the great script of history—the actions of ordinary people are often forgotten. In the most dramatic of times, Bruna proved to have determination and courage that perhaps even she did not know she possessed. During the hectic times of war, in which the selfishness of many is amplified, she risked her own life to save the lives of others.

Bruna, wherever you are—either on earth or in heaven—I have endless admiration for you, and I am immensely grateful for everything you did for my father and uncle.

ESCAPING FROM THE CAMP

Being in possession of the stamped permits, Giulio and Renato waited patiently for the opportunity to escape. Once again, good luck came their way. After a few days, an Austrian commander came to the camp and met the Salani brothers, and they made a good impression on him with their kindness.

He later came to them in secret and said he would be guarding the gates at dawn the next morning. That would be the perfect time to get away. This officer had been pretending to be on the Germans' side, but he was actually helping prisoners. Back in Austria, Germans had murdered his wife and entire family, and then burned his house and pipe factory down.

Everything was in place for their escape. However, the two brothers hesitated—could they trust this officer? Was his hatred for the Germans genuine? Was he really willing to help two prisoners, exposing himself to such serious risk? Or was it a trap?

It was their fate to leave, though. That night (November 28th-29th), the camp was heavily bombed by British airplanes, leaving part of the barbed wire fence destroyed. Many prisoners were able to escape that night, and among them were Giulio and Renato.

The former kitchen of Fossoli camp after the bombing on November 29th, 1944.

The shacks of the camp after the bombing.

Renato wrote a farewell in his DIARY:

It was six o'clock and we saluted
the nets, the walls, the camp ... everything speaks;
they send us their wishes and we go,
remembering the sad farewell to Nina and Carla.

But the saddest far more painful salute was the one
that our dearest friend gave us;
brother and friend together was our Nullo,
a farewell soaked by sincere tears.

Weaving praises about him is not my job:
(I admire) his personality, goodness, good health,
he's not ugly:
he is an accountant, but he understands very well,
I sublimate his spirit and there is still more to say.

The brothers ran and kicked up their legs, the heels of their shoes pounding against the ground, fleeing. They were afraid they would be caught by the Germans; they ran as fast as their legs would allow them. Once they were free from the vicinity of the camp, there was a long walk ahead of them, and it was early winter. Even then, MUSIC came to their rescue, relieving their fatigue and driving away their fears. They harmonized a tune and maintained a constant, steady pace.

This way, a dense fog accompanies us
all along the long run for that valley.
We enjoy the beauty of the countryside,
the weight of backpacks on our shoulders.

Fortunately, in the craziness of the escape, they had not forgotten to take with them all of the essential things: Uncle Renato's TOILET PAPER DIARY, photos taken in the camp, some bread, a few personal garments, their wages from typewriting, and above all, their documents—the precious permits with the German commander's stamp.

After many hours of walking, they arrived in Mirandola. From there they took the courier (a bus), until they reached San Martino Spino.

Their imprisonment had lasted almost four months—from August 10th to November 29th, 1944. Uncle Renato had promised to have my Father Giulio home by Christmas, and he had kept that promise. Again, numb13 had brought luck!

When we boarded the bus,
we aroused feelings of pity as well as compassion.
To Giulio, I prophesied and reassured:
Do not fear, for luck will find us

As soon as Renato and Giulio arrived at San Martino Spino, they visited their relatives, Aunt Sara and their Cousins Adriano and Laura, who had come to them while they were imprisoned in the camp. Their cousin Adriano took the brothers to Mass in the same church where Euclide grew up, where the whole village gathered around at the front of the church, waiting to welcome and embrace the children of Maestro Euclide Salani.

This was the San Martino Spino Parish Church, where Luigi Salani, the "bell-ringer" lived and where Euclide grew up as a young man.

They played and sang the Ave Maria by Schubert and other liturgical hymns, with Renato at the organ and Giulio at the violin.

This is the organ at the San Martino Spino Parish Church.

We arrived on time
to our dear father's hometown ...

I cannot tell you the relatives' welcome:
I do not hide a bit of emotion.
Everyone, everybody was happy that day,
we all praised FREEDOM.

And though freedom was all we wanted,
we missed the freedoms of having a job.
But for the roses and the flowers,
I thanked our Saint in Heaven.

I have to tell you, though, that day
when the city's patron was celebrated,
with Dad's friends, there all around me,
I was playing in church ... sacred hymns.

Giulio and I played
in the Church of St. Martino and later in Pilastri.
A jam of people in the sacristy: eh, what do they want?
Everyone is anxious to hear these two STARS!!!

How modest, am I not? There is no harm.
But listen: it was just like that,
because it was extraordinary, the many lunches
and love that each one offered to us.

Besides inviting them to lunch, the villagers donated sweaters, underpants, and coats to the Salani brothers; in short, they restored them—refreshing them and dressing them properly.

Soon, news arrived of another bombing at the Fossoli concentration camp, and it was learned that the surviving prisoners had been transferred to Gonzaga in the Mantova area.

... Do you know that after we left they bombed the camp again? Killing four or five friends of ours, poor things!!! I'm so sorry,
and I mourn and sympathize with their grieving families.

After the celebrations and high emotions of family reunion, their relatives became cautious. Giulio and Renato were still fugitives, so giving them refuge was very dangerous. If the Germans discovered that they were hiding them, they would be shot. The Salani brothers did not want to jeopardize the lives of their relatives, so they left San Martino Spino and went to Maranello.

When they arrived, they happened to see a convoy of German trucks going to Pievepelago. Renato made a decision. With his heart hammering in his chest, my uncle showed their permits to the officers in charge and asked for a ride, saying they were going to visit their relatives. They held their breath while the German officer examined the documents. He looked over them for a moment, then returned the stamped permits and let them get on. It worked!

They arrived at Pievepelago and Renato began to think about his mother:

My dear mom, writing this letter, I'm thinking about you:
we have already arrived to Pievepelago,
and we've been staying here for about three days:
we want to try to get home ... Will we get lucky?

I still see you, I know, but you're always crying,
in the dark or turquoise sky.
Those who you are already mourning,
will soon be near and beside you.

Smile, Mommy, look happy:
so that my heart is right and content.

*Soon you will see us, and that vision
can lift you, with certainty from all your sufferings.*

*Come on, erase from your face that terrible dismay!
Look at us... and tell us if we are looking good.
We were at the concentration camp
and later at San Martino Spino.*

Chapter 12
THE CROSSING OF THE APENNINE MOUNTAINS

Using the money they had earned by working in the office at the Fossoli camp, the two brothers decided to hire guides to cross the Tosco-Emilian Apennines, a 59 mile trip across the snowy mountains on treacherous terrain with no designated routes. Most of the roads and bridges were destroyed by the bombings. [8]

(You can see all the distances hereafter with Google Maps on the sitography).

From Pievepelago Uncle Renato walked to a neighboring town, Sant'Annapelago, to look for guides. [9]

As did Gisto (a friend of theirs from Viareggio), he went to Tagliole, but neither of them found a guide. [10]

> *We prepare and get ready for departing,*
> *looking first in Sant'Anna*
> *for a guide that, with good competence,*
> *will take us over the mountains.*

On the morning of the third day of searching for guides, my father went to Rotari, a village farther away. [11]
He returned late in the afternoon, after walking for nine hours, very tired, but happy: he had found some guides who had accepted their engagement. However, they wanted to be paid the same amount again for the return trip, and they wanted to bring along some other guides who lived in a distant town. Giulio and Renato accepted all their conditions and went on their way to get the other guides.

Gisto looks up there at Tagliole,
and Giulio finds them instead at Rotari;
he returns to us saying: "Hey, guys we can go now
there are no Germans nearby, we can cross."

Trying to find the help of the guides,
Giulio went up and down the mountains all day.
They had their conditions:
you must pay for our return.

Okay, okay! Whatever you want!
You will be given without any reticence;
If we count on you, will you help us?
So, they asked us to get ready for the departure.

We saluted Pievepelago,
where we felt so good and comfortable:
We want to go, we have a lake nearby our house, too;
we want to leave, we are very tired.

While we were climbing up the mountains,
on our way to the guide's mountain cottage;
Giulio went ahead to ensure our safety,
returning to say: "You can trust me".

Two and a half hours on the mule track,
we walked to the village,
arriving late into the night,
in which two people had an adverse destiny.

Exhausted and hungry, they arrived at the village where the second guides lived. Looking around, they spotted a wedding party. (The bride was pregnant, so it was a called a "repairing wedding"...)

*Oh! Don't worry, don't be impressed,
and it shows the reason for the party ...*

*In a few words, marriage was made
to give parents to that boy,
of whom the embryo was already growing
in the womb of the bride, his mother.*

What a joy to be in the middle of that party! The prospect of playing, singing, and dancing overwhelmed their fatigue. My dad asked if they could join the wedding feast, and in return, they would play and sing for the guests. So yet again, MUSIC came to their rescue, giving them an opportunity to eat a good meal—exactly what they needed after a long, hard day of walking, and a longer, harder expedition ahead of them.

The two brothers gave their all: Uncle Renato played the accordion, while Giulio sang and danced exuberantly. That night, all their anxieties disappeared—they were no longer afraid of their unknown futures. Music is the real moonlight in the dark night of life.

*There was such a great gala that night,
where we happened to be just by chance.
I played the accordion in the middle of the room
And we drank cups of fine quality wine.*

*Giulio danced his heart out all evening,
his spirit soaring high;
he danced without thinking and after a while
it was time to cross the mountains.*

At the end of the party, with full stomachs and sleepy eyes, they wanted nothing but a good sleep. Instead, they could not rest for a moment; the full moon was lighting up the path in the snow-capped mountains, and the guides insisted on leaving immediately. Traveling by night, the risk of running into a German patrol was negligible, so shortly before midnight, they set off, prepared to walk until dawn.

*At half past eleven we left,
thinking and hoping that soon we would arrive.
The hike was hard, the crossing long,
Beginning with minimal effort, but the rest ...*

The snow was high and they proceeded with difficulty. Unlike the guides, Renato and Giulio were not wearing mountain boots, but normal city shoes. When Uncle Renato slipped and fell behind, he shouted for them to come back and wait for him. The guides came back, but immediately said, "Do you want the Germans to kill us all? If you shout like that, they will find and catch us!" My uncle replied jokingly, "Well... If I have to die, I do not want to die alone—I prefer to die in company!"

I started such a steep climb that I bet,
it is impossible to guess just how high;
all of them were ahead of me and for this reason,
I started to yell very loudly!

Most of them had well-worn mountain boots,
so that it was easier for them to walk;
climbing the steep slope ... Oh lucky legs:
they left me alone behind, hoping I would get moving...

Despite their fatigue and the difficulty of the path in the high snow, Giulio and Renato could not help but admire the sublime spectacle of nature, with snow-covered trees glittering in the moon's glow.

> *Beautiful scenery! .... And the moon*
> *reflecting its rays on the snow.*
> *I saw myself lost when one of the guides,*
> *helped me briefly.*
>
> *But it was difficult to climb;*
> *too difficult for us who were so unprepared.*
> *A mountain ... and another well-frozen one,*
> *had lined up leading us into despair.*

The trip seemed endless. At the top of a mountain, they couldn't even take the time to catch their breath or celebrate their accomplishment, for up ahead, there was another peak; and then yet another one. When they came across steep and icy trails, the guides made small holes in the snow with their boots to help those worse equipped for and less accustomed to the wintery terrain.

At one point, they came to a basin in the middle of two mountains, where a strong, icy wind was blowing; they felt as if the wind was cutting their ears. Uncle Renato looked in his backpack for something to cover his head, but found only underpants. Nevertheless, he put them on his head: anything to protect him from the biting cold wind. It had to have been an amusing sight, but no one had enough strength left to laugh.

Finally, one last peak stood in front of them—steep, covered with immaculate snow, and completely treeless.

It was the most terrible, the final one;
The tallest ... all white up there ...
It was a challenge ... in front of us
 and right here it was ... that Giulio fell down!

Chapter 13
GIULIO

This chapter is dedicated to my dad, with endless gratitude and love, for I have never known such a generous, kind, good, and altruistic man. Dad, you are a legend, my great hero!

Always ready to sacrifice himself for the good of many, my father, for me, is the truest example of honor, dignity, respect, and courage. He was also a very handsome young man: tall and slender, and fascinating with his refined and serene ways. He spoke four languages and, as I have already mentioned, had graduated as a junior accountant. After the war, he received his PhD in economics and business from the University of Pisa, quite an achievement for those days...

But for now, let's go back to where we were at the end of the previous chapter—that is, on the snowy Tosco-Emilian Apennines, walking the arduous road that would lead Renato and Giulio to freedom.

Utterly exhausted from two days of walking on steep mountain trails, my father fell to the ground.

> *Oh, what a dismay in everyone's hearts!*
> *To everyone in the group.*
> *Eh! Certainly, this was a serious moment ...*
> *and could compromise the crossing.*

My father could not get up. "Go," he said to his companions, "I cannot walk, I can't do it anymore!"

Uncle Renato stopped to help him, but the guides insisted on continuing, threatening to leave Giulio there to die of starvation and weather exposure. Two of the guides lifted my father and started dragging him up the mountain. Soon, however, they stopped and told him, "If you do not have the strength to walk, we cannot go any further, because you are endangering not just your own life but the lives of all of us."

Uncle Renato offered them the last 6,000 *lire* he had in his backpack. The money persuaded the guides to help him again, but not for much longer. After a short while, they abandoned Giulio on the ground and left.

Here, Uncle Renato recalls the anguish of that moment:

They helped him once, twice ... three times;
he seemed to me like a Jesus Christ on the Calvary...
And he fell once more ... and a guide told me:
- this is it, that's the path.

And they showed us the way
that would take us to the other mountainside;
and they left me with poor Giulio,
exhausted in the snow; until when?

Renato worked really hard to revive his brother. He found a piece of dry bread in his backpack, softened it with a bit of clean snow, and put it in Giulio's mouth, hoping to restore some of his energy. He reminded him that their mom was at home waiting for them, and that he could not remain here, for he would die. "Get up, our mom is waiting for us to spend Christmas together!"

Giulio's love for his mom, and the desire to spend Christmas together with the whole family, was the inner push he needed to give him the strength to stand up and walk—without stopping and without eating—for four more hours.

> *As soon as I told him: Giulio, listen:*
> *our mom is there waiting for us,*
> *and she hopes to see all of our family*
> *gathering at Christmas and New Year's.*
>
> *And pray the Virgin Mary without ceasing*
> *to give us her blessing;*
> *during all the walking we have left,*
> *she sends us her protection.*

*As soon as I said that, in a flash Giulio got up,
and for four hours without rest,
he walked up those snowy mountains
arriving to the Allied military outpost.*

*A grace, a Miracle, I say;
how can we otherwise explain?!
Thank you, Madonna and thank you, God,
I will light a big candle in the altar.*

After four hours, which seemed like four centuries to them, they saw a chalet with a fire where shepherds lived. They stopped, dried their snowy and wet clothes, restored themselves, and rested a little. After some time, they went back walking, hoping to find the camps of Allied troops. Without the guides, they were almost blind in that foreign territory. Finally, after passing several more peaks, they arrived at Fornaci di Barga and found the American troops!

*Fornaci di Barga, delightful small town
on the fresh mountains of Garfagnana
welcomed us ... and here we encountered
the Fifth American Contingent.*

They asked: Who are you, where are you going?
We're going home, can't you see?
We were prisoners, we were raided
by the Germans ... you know...

We want to go to Viareggio, oh, how brilliant!
Or maybe to Massaciuccoli by our grandparents'
Instead they took us to Florence
to the Refugee Center to soothe our needs.

The brothers explained to the US soldiers who they were and what their goal was. They had burned the papers from the concentration camp to avoid giving embarrassing explanations about permits stamped by a Nazi officer.

Fornaci di Barga—in the province of Lucca—is near Massaciuccoli, so Giulio and Renato had hoped to be able to go home soon. Instead, the Americans made them get on a truck to Florence. This worried them: were they escaping from the Germans only to end up as prisoners of the Americans? Fortunately, their fears turned out to be unfounded, because in Florence, they were housed in a refugee center. They were welcomed warmly, but the food was terrible. Only slop was given, which restored them very little. With the hunger, they had from crossing the snow-capped Apennine Mountains on foot, a little soup was not going to satiate their appetites. On the bright side, though, at least the soup was hot!

They were also given orange jumpsuits to wear (the uniform of the refugee camp), instead of the sopping wet clothes they had on during all those days.

Chapter 14
FINALLY, FREE!

The Tuscan resistance was relatively short compared to that of the north; the southern region was liberated by the end of 1944. Nevertheless, among the fighters and patriots, the Tuscans active in the resistance were almost 30,000. Moreover, for the first time since the beginning of the Italian campaign, the Allies faced a well-organized political and military movement in Tuscany. In June of 1944, a committee made up of anti-fascist parties, the Tuscan National Liberation Committee (TNLC), proclaimed the partisan forces to be the legitimate governing bodies of the region, telling them to take control of the liberated cities and establish an Italian administration. The goal was achieved, as in the case of Florence, on August 11th, 1944, despite the Allies ordering the partisans to disarm the week before. The order was soon revoked, as the partisans were threatening to oppose the Allies with force.

In Florence, the Salani brothers were finally enjoying freedom, as they had crossed the front. In fact, the Americans had already freed that area from German hegemony, so they could safely get out of the refugee camp. After a while, they were able to go out and enjoy serene walks, no longer burdened by the fear of being caught or having to return at a certain time. One day, while walking around the city, it started to rain. They retreated under the *loggia* of a palace, waiting for the thunderstorm to soften a little. Suddenly, they heard a friendly voice, "Renato, what are you doing here?!" Uncle Renato turned and recognized his dear friend Boschi, a musician who played the first saxophone in the Navy Orchestra when he was a soldier.

> *We met Boschi under a loggia*
> *of a palace in Florence,*
> *a way to shelter us from the rainstorm,*
> *fortunately, we entered under that main door.*

What a great joy! What a happy meeting! Chance and luck had brought them together under the same *loggia* during a storm, of all things. Boschi informed Renato that he was playing the saxophone in an orchestra at the Alhambra Hotel in Florence, and that they were looking for a good pianist. He asked Renato if he wanted to audition.

It was Boschi, I repeat, the one who introduced me
to his friends who needed
a good pianist ... and I have to boast
saying that, I can sight read pretty well.

The proposal intrigued my uncle, but after five months away, he first wanted to go home and be with his family.

He told Boschi the ordeals he experienced with Giulio in the concentration camp and promised him that after spending Christmas with his family, he would return to Florence as the pianist of the orchestra. He also pointed out that he was still wearing the orange uniform from the refugee center—he was certainly not dressed for a performance! Boschi, however, insisted, "I will give you elegant clothes. Go ahead. Do the audition!"

One morning, we went for the audition
at the Alhambra, Giulio and I... What an emotion!
The room was beautiful and ... How much food
on those tables sumptuously laid!

How hungry we were!
Oh man, we would have eaten everything,
oh, me unfortunate!
But no! I cannot do anything
for that brioche that fell there, under the table!

I introduced myself to those new friends, who,
with impatience, were waiting for the audition of
the pianist; "have you heard Tu che m'hai preso il cuor?
It sounds like it is not new for you."

*In fact, I played that song and many others, like
"Mattinata Fiorentina" liking those gentlemen
who had something to say, they told me:
"If you want, you can start right now:
you will earn with us six hundred liras."*

The pay was good and Renato gladly accepted.

*Six hundred liras a day, of course I'll go!
If compared to the thousand per month
that I earned within the concentration camp,
when they paid me always reluctantly.*

*I'm sure I'll accept it, but I'll come back
after I get to hug my parents,
who have been waiting for my return for months
as well as my brother's, the two younger children.*

*I will return to you after Christmas,
because I promised my family a long time ago,
I'd meet them at my grandfather's farm
at Massaciuccoli, gathering all together.*

*So, we went back to the Refugee Center
to drink a little bit of that "puddle" soup,
preparing all our documents ... And we found
a wagon that looked like a "Flagship".*

*We crossed Prato, Pistoia and Montecatini,
we travelled without pausing a moment,
we passed Lucca and as pilgrims,
at sunset, finally we arrived home.*

On the site www. 4loveofmusic.com you can listen to *Il Potpourri Italiano* where the song *Mattinata Fiorentina*, is included, arranged by Renato Salani and sung by Giulio Salani.

Chapter 15
THE ARRIVAL HOME

At last, on December 11th, 1944, Renato and Giulio arrived home to their grandparents' (Gesualda and Giulio) country house in Massaciuccoli.

There they found their whole family—dad, mom, grandparents, sisters, and all their relatives—who had been displaced from Viareggio during the war. Grandma Maria was so overwhelmed with joy on seeing Renato and Giulio that she could not even speak—she just held them and cried. Even though the war was not entirely over, the Salanis spent a happy and cheerful Christmas together. There was lots of music and laughter as the family was finally reunited. Further north, however, families would have to wait until next Christmas for a happy celebration.

Everyone was there! Grandparents, cousins, mom, dad, uncles, aunts and sisters:
hugs, kisses .... Tears ... And a range
of good wines, sweets and candies.

What a feast, what a delight, what a joy this was:
we spoke to everyone and all were happy:
how beautiful my family has always been!
With my grandfather, the best of my relatives.

O grandpa, I loved you so much
because you were always good to me.
You always caressed me ....
And your heart was always moved
by listening to the sounds of the music I played.

Finally, after Christmas, the Salani family, after the evacuation order was revoked, could return to their home in Viareggio. From the left: Elsa, Euclide, Renato, Olga, their cousin Italo, Ada, and Giulio in front of their home.

Renato spoke to his father of his possible position as a musician in Florence, but his father was not convinced ...

*So, I talked to my dad on those evenings
how and why should I sign that contract.
"Not a musician." he cried, "You're an accountant!
Why do you do these things, are you crazy?"*

*Well, yes Dad, I know, I'm an accountant,
but I like music and you know
that I am not cut to that craft;
allow me to play, please.*

*We talked a lot, then finally he said:
"You are already older so you have to
do what you feel ..." and he said to me:
"Always study and practice hard, so you'll never have trouble!"*

Renato listened carefully to his father's words and did "what he felt": music called him in Florence. "Dad," he said, "this is the accounting diploma that you wanted me to earn. Now, let me decide what I want to do with my life: I want to devote it to music!"

Euclide probably did not approve, but certainly, deep in his soul, he understood: for he too, was a musician...

When he departed for Florence, Renato had to make the 72-mile journey by bicycle, the only means of transportation in Tuscany, where neither bridges nor rail lines were in operation. He spent an entire day riding, even crossing through rivers with the bike held high on his shoulders.

Once in Florence, Renato worked with the band for the Alhambra Hotel during the evenings; during the day, he did arrangements for the orchestras of Maestro Cinico Angelini and Francesco Ferrari, performing on the RAI (Italian Radio).

Renato Salani at the piano with the Alhambra Hotel orchestra.

Here we can see Renato at the piano with the orchestra in Florence, where American and British officers went to have fun in the evenings.

The Alhambra Hotel Orchestra in Florence

Meanwhile, Giulio, at 19 and living in Viareggio, began playing with the orchestra directed by Loredano Santini, a well-known pianist and his dear friend. He would perform in the evenings in Versilia, as well as in other famous and popular places across Italy and Europe.

Giulio playing the clarinet in Loredano Santini's Orchestra.

He also enrolled in the School of Economics and Business at Pisa University, keeping up with his studies and supporting them with his musical earnings. When he would start playing music again, he would forget the world, his worries, and would be overwhelmed by the whirlwind of notes that rose towards the sky.

Chapter 16
The S-13 ORCHESTRA and TRIO ALBA

When his contract at the Alhambra Hotel ended, Renato decided to create his own band with three well-known musicians in Florence: Labardi, the bassist; Costanzo, the drummer; and Dondero, on the trumpet. Renato, in homage to his lucky number, decided to call his band "S-13" (Salani 13). Still, his lucky number stayed true: after just a few days, the Viareggio Municipal Casino offered a four-year contract to S-13.

Renato Salani's S-13 orchestra.

S-13 Orchestra performing at the *Principe di Piemonte* Hotel and Casino in Viareggio.

In addition to playing during the weekend evenings at the Viareggio Principe di Piemonte Hotel and Casino with the S-13, Renato tried to please his father Euclide as well. He got a job at the Commercial Bank of Viareggio, and for a period of time he tried to combine the unstable job of a musician with the secure and steady one of a banker. This only lasted a short time, however, "I see the notes in place of the numbers," Renato recalls. For this reason, he resigned and forever abandoned his banking career.

I was pleased with healthy living:
I made so many beautiful arrangements.
One day, who did I see? It was Germana!
She had come to congratulate me.

As a boy, Renato had feelings for Germana, a pretty young girl. However, their relationship was complicated and Germana was difficult to get along with as she had a temper and often had a negative attitude. Then the war came, and they drifted further apart. When, after many years, she walked into the room where he was playing, Renato's heart skipped a beat, "It's not possible ... It's Germana!" She also recognized him immediately and congratulated him on his performance. The two youngsters soon became involved again— they had so many things to tell each other! Just a short time after, they were engaged.

And soon I started courting her,
talking about the past and the war;
in a short time, we got engaged
believing that heaven had landed on Earth!

Three years of drama and suffering,
it ended up leaving us broken hearted:
what good is it, Germana, all your knowledge of science if you're always crying and live embittered?

During the carnival, the Viareggio Principe di Piemonte Hotel and Casino hired Trio Alba, a singing group comprised of the Scalzitti sisters: Nancy, Anna Maria, and Alma, who were often accompanied by S-13 orchestra.

From the left: Nancy, Anna Maria, and Alma, at Viareggio in 1946.

Trio Alba performing at the Royal Hotel during the Carnival of Viareggio in 1948.

Trio Alba in Milan.

Trio Alba at the Viareggio Principe di Piemonte Hotel and Casino in 1948. From the Left: Alma, Anna Maria, and Nancy.

While Renato was living his long-suffering love story with Germana, Giulio met Nancy, the soprano voice at Trio Alba—it was love at first sight, and they were soon engaged.

Nancy and Giulio when they met.

Giulio Salani and Nancy Scalzitti when they got engaged and their engagement lasted for 5 years while Giulio attended the University of Pisa.

Nancy was born in New York, where her father, my Grandfather Filiberto Scalzitti, worked as a mechanical engineer on the construction of the subway. Nancy was 18 months old when Filiberto became ill and expressed the desire to return to Italy to see his relatives. His wife, Felicita, gladly agreed, so they moved back to Italy with their three little girls: Diva, Anna Maria, and Nancy. Alma was born in Viareggio a few months later.

Nancy was a jovial person, and had an open, honest, and generous character. Giulio was confident that their union would be happy and was delighted by their music and peaceful relationship—a result of the compatibility of their personalities. "Two things save us in life: love and laugh. If you have one, okay. If you have both of them, you are invincible," says Indian writer Tarun Tejpal. Love is really an immeasurable force.

Giulio and Nancy happily riding a moped.

Meanwhile, Sergio Bernardini, a widely known club owner and artist manager in Versilia, had purchased the ballroom "Il Gatto Nero". He had known the Salanis since childhood, so he went to the Municipal Casino at the Principe di Piemonte Hotel in Viareggio and offered to hire Renato and S-13 for the summer season. Renato accepted his offer, and, because Giulio often joined S-13 when he was home between other musical contracts, the brothers found themselves in the surreal position of returning to the Gatto Nero Night Club - no longer as cigar vendors, but as the main entertainments act as musicians.

This 1951 photo shows Renato Salani's S-13 orchestra. They're playing at the Gatto Nero Dancing Club with customers dancing at Viareggio's Pineta (Pinewood park). Giulio Salani (standing) is playing his tenor sax.

For the two brothers, it was a hectic year. When the summer season ended in Versilia, Giulio packed his bags and was called to perform in several cities in Italy and Europe:

Venice, Portofino, Sanremo, Turin, Florence, Rome, Garmisch Partenkirchen, and Munich, among others, where he also played jazz in the Marienplatz (a central square in Munich, Germany) for a live audience and for the radio. Besides singing, Giulio played his three favorite instruments: clarinet, saxophone, and violin.

In 1950, Giulio had a series of gigs in Florence where he had the opportunity to play with the famous trumpet player Bill Coleman, pictured.

Bill Coleman listens, amused, while Giulio plays the clarinet.

Bill Coleman's dedication to Giulio: "To Salani Giulio, it was great working with you. Sincerely, Bill Coleman.

Giulio (third from left) playing the tenor sax in the Lotti Orchestra in Rome for a TV show.

The complete Maestro Lotti's orchestra. The second sax from the right is Giulio Salani.

This show on RAI television was hosted by Mario Riva, the famous Italian TV host and actor, in his black tuxedo on the left.

Giulio Salani at Garmisch Partenkirchen.

While working at the casino in Venice, Giulio met and accompanied (on the clarinet) the famous American actress, singer, and swimmer, Esther Williams. She showered him with compliments, and told him that he reminded her of the great Italian American clarinet player Buddy De Franco.

As if that wasn't enough, Giulio also spent hours and hours studying for his economics courses, and was able to regularly take his exams at the University of Pisa. Even with all these commitments, he did not neglect Nancy, with whom he spent his (brief) spare time.

Nancy and Giulio relaxing at the beach in Viareggio, the Perl of the Tyrrhenian Sea.

Giulio and Nancy dining in a restaurant.

Here they are dancing.

Renato often accompanied Giulio to the Trio Alba sisters' home to teach the girls their new vocal arrangements. Vocal trios were very popular during the postwar period, and the best known was probably the Andrew Sisters in the USA. Renato appreciated the talent of Trio Alba and made a commitment to arrange their songs, helping them to achieve great success!

(Left) The program for *Il Pino nell'Orto*, performed by Renato Salani with S-13 and Trio Alba. (Right) Nancy as a soloist during a live broadcast program on the radio.

Nancy Scalzitti receiving flowers from her fans after her soloist performance.

After his summer contracts in Versilia, Renato was working in Turin, and when Giulio arrived for a visit, Renato asked him for a huge favor. He handed him a birthday gift he had gotten Germana (who was living in Carrara at the time), and begged him to deliver it for him along with a bunch of red roses.

*From Turin, I entrusted
my brother to go to Carrara;
but he sent Alma, he was busy,
he had exams at the University ...*

Giulio had all the good intentions to fulfill his brother's request, but he had an exam. Nancy was also busy with her work, so he entrusted the gift to young Alma, who was more than happy to enjoy a train trip from Viareggio to Carrara. She delivered Renato's gift to Germana, though for the red roses, she could only relay his thoughts and intention to deliver flowers—Alma had not been able to find any, as it was not the right season. Renato and Germana were still engaged, but he was already considering letting her go and breaking up with her due to the continued drama. After a while, their painful and tormented love story came to the end...

At www.4loveofmusic.com, you can listen to *Boogie Boo* and *Cip Cip*, masterfully arranged and played by Renato Salani's band, and interpreted by Trio Alba.

Chapter 17
ALMA AND RENATO

As Renato traveled continuously for work, he had the opportunity to meet many nice and beautiful women. However, he was especially attracted to Alma, the youngest member of Trio Alba, who was blossoming into a gorgeous young woman. Mother Maria also pointed this out to him. "Have you seen how cute Alma is?" she asked him one day.

I'll let Uncle Renato's DIARY speak for him about Alma:

In fact, in a cool spring day,
high heels, a nice red coat,
a ponytail: "Oh God, who was that?"
I saw something I wasn't expecting.

Alma, is that you? But... I do not recognize you!
With that coat, that skirt!
You are different from how I know you,
is that really you? My God! What a beautiful lady!

*If you have no commitments at this time
I'll run and cancel mine,
I'll tell them I'm not available, and,
we will go for a walk to la Passeggiata.*

*But yesterday, you were still a little girl!
How did you change so much?
I taught you how to sing ... you were a kid,
I feel like publishing your photo in the newspaper!*

Later, they officially got engaged. You can see them dancing at the Gatto Nero Club in the photo.
Renato was playing the piano as the leader of his orchestra S-13, and during the break, he proposed!

*Is it possible that, in such a long time,
after coming to sing in my house,
I had never thought before,
that you were created to become my dear wife?*

*I did not think about it because at twenty-three years old
I wasn't thinking of any fourteen-year old girl;
there are other skirts, other dresses,
take the example that the Nordic people give us...*

*And then, there are girls who are already beautiful,
they are already well-developed at that age;
you weren't, you've never been like those girls,
when you were twenty you showed your curves...*

*But believe me, that way it was better;
it seemed that you were there waiting for me,
waiting for me to wake up,
to come to you declaring me.*

*One thing that I'm sure of:
You did not think, that the man
with whom you would divide your future,
could be me, your vocal maestro.*

I have already said it, but now I repeat it:
I am glad I met you,
You filled my world completely,
You were my Grace received.

What else should I say that would bring
respect and dignity to my wife,
for the simplicity with which she raised
my spirit to poetry!

<u>A</u>mazing mother of my children
<u>L</u>ove me unconditionally
<u>M</u>aintain me away from troubles
<u>A</u>lways God testifies the precious goodness.

I write to you four lines, dear Almetta,
to tell you that I was lucky
to meet you and have you as wife,
perfect woman for such a complicated man.

You are a great wife and friend:
as mom ... absolutely exceptional!
when we got married, the big drums played
and the wedding lunch was at the
Pini sul Viale.

Alma and Renato married on October 4th, 1952.

Alma and Renato Salani at the reception of their wedding at the "Pini sul Viale" restaurant.

HONEYMOON

*In the evening we left for Paris,
thinking about doing the best things well done.*

*The Seine, the boulevards and the big sky ...
We were looking forward to seeing it ...
But it was as cloudy as Turin!*

*We passed the first night of the wedding ...
What a delicacy! What a refined creature
I found between these rough hands ...
And I went happily towards my fate ...*

Three handsome boys were the outcome of their great love: (left to right) Stefano, Riccardo, and Andrea. All three graduated as engineers.

Chapter 18
THE SANREMO FESTIVAL

On returning from their honeymoon, inspired by his love for Alma, Renato wrote the song *No Pierrot*, which was presented at the 1953 Sanremo Festival (also known as the Festival of the Italian Song) in Florence by Edizioni Da Rovere.

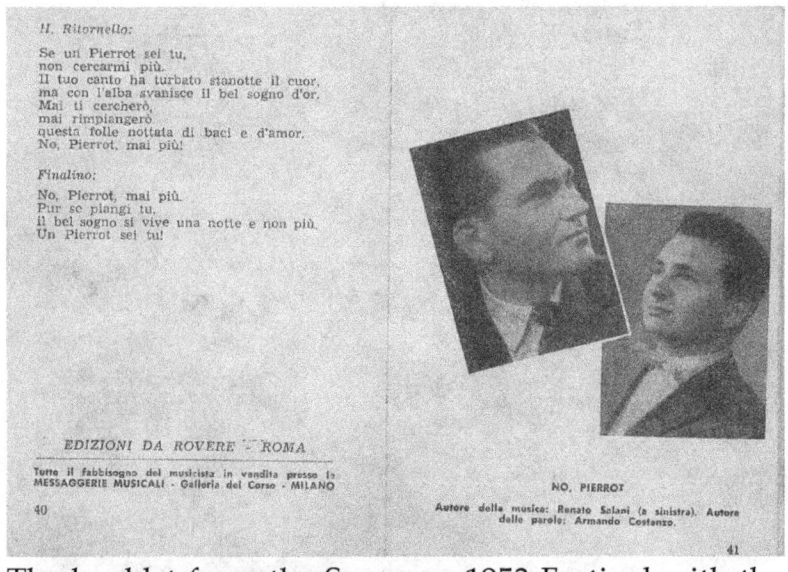

The booklet from the Sanremo 1953 Festival with the lyrics of the song *No Pierrot*. The pictures are of the composer of the music, Renato Salani and the author of the lyrics, Armando Costanzo.

From January 29th to 31st, 1953, *No Pierrot* was performed by two artists with two different orchestras and arrangements (as per the rules of the festival—each song had to be performed twice by different artists). This festival tradition was maintained until 1971, when other rules were introduced, forever taking away from the atmosphere of the first two festivals. A traditional arrangement of *No Pierrot* was directed by the veteran Maestro Cinico Angelini, and the modern version by Armando Trovajoli, a jazz enthusiast. The media of the time did not let go of the opportunity to emphasize rivalry, true or not, between the two masters.

Renato's song was given to singers Katyna Ranieri and Achille Togliani, who came to the final and won the sixth place.

By visiting our website: www.4loveofmusic.com you can see the actual record of the song *No Pierrot*: You can hear both Katyna Ranieri's version, as well as Achille Togliani's version of *No Pierrot* by Renato Salani. Enjoy it!

The *libretto* of the songs performed at the Sanremo Festival in 1953.

Chapter 19
GIULIO AND NANCY

A DEGREE, A SECURE JOB, and NOSTALGIA FOR MUSIC.

Finally, on November 15th, 1951, Giulio was honored with his degree: a Doctorate in Economics and Business from Pisa University!

Giulio's diploma.

Following the advice of his father, he decided to apply for a job at a bank, and he was soon hired at a bank in Milan, where he worked for a couple of years. In the evenings, however, after having worked all day, he did not feel satisfied; he was missing something. He took his instruments (particularly his clarinet) and went to play jazz in ballrooms with musicians from other bands. His degree was important, his job at the bank was secure, but he had to play! He could not live without making music.

Music had created a glimmer in the sky for Giulio.

As Marco Tullio Cicero once said, "A life without music is like a soulless body."

I think Cicero's phrase fits perfectly with my father. For eight to ten hours a day he lived without a soul, but was magically reunited with it as soon as his fingers were dancing on his beloved clarinet.

He still intended to follow his father's advice, though, and understood Euclide was right when he said, "It's better to work at a bank than to make a living as a musician; it's better to have a fixed place and a safe salary than to run here and there, always on the go, hoping for a contract that who knows when it will arrive."

Giulio could only agree: a fixed salary would secure him the economic stability needed to marry Nancy.

He continued working in Milan, but returned to Viareggio as soon as he could, to visit Nancy and enjoy the sea and the beach with her.

Giulio reading a book at the beach—melancholy, and staring thoughtfully at the sea.

Naturally, Nancy knew that Giulio was not satisfied with his job. She often saw him thoughtful and restless, so she gave him a push, telling him to follow his true vocation. Nancy understood perfectly that Giulio had worked in the bank so he could afford to marry her, and he had continued to work there to guarantee her economic security.

Nancy Scalzitti.

She understood equally well that Giulio's dissatisfaction was a shadow over their happiness, so she told him sincerely that she wanted to be married to a musician; she would always support his choice and share any sacrifices that must be made with him. She did not want his bank account, she wanted a happy husband.

THEIR MARRIAGE

Music begins where the words end ... And with music begins love ... Music is the mediator between spiritual and sensual life.
—Ludwig van Beethoven

Giulio and Nancy had met by making music together; they were two souls born for each other, who showed us the importance of family, love, morality, goodness, music, happiness, and the knowledge that you're never alone. I stand on the solid foundations of my parents' affection and esteem for one another, and I thank God that I am so fortunate to have this family and my wonderful parents, who loved each other unfailingly, even until their last breaths.

Nancy and Giulio married in Viareggio, after five years of engagement.

Giulio and Nancy the day of their wedding, April 27th, 1953.

Renato and Alma at Nancy and Giulio's wedding.

Subsequently, Giulio followed his dream and began working all over Europe as a musician, taking on several six-month contracts. This time, Nancy was part of that dream and together they lived in Turin, Milan, Sanremo, Lido di Venezia and many other cities.

Giulio and Nancy at Fontana di Trevi in Rome, Italy.

Giulio and Nancy in Santa Marinella, Rome.

Nancy and Giulio are in Frascati, Rome, Italy.

And here they are in Milan, Italy.

Nancy and Giulio in Geneva, Switzerland.

And here in Lucerne, Switzerland.

My mom told me that they had to make great sacrifices at that time, for example, instead of going to a restaurant, they would enjoy picnics in parks, sharing sandwiches and a glass of wine. They were so happy to be together, though, that these sacrifices were inconsequential.

Soon Renato called Giulio to join his band, and this was the start of a wonderful era: the quartet of two brothers married to two sisters went around Europe playing and singing, always living in harmony.

Chapter 20
FRED BUSCAGLIONE AND THE ASTERNOVAS ORCHESTRA

After the end of the war, the renowned musician and songwriter Fred Buscaglione returned to his hometown in Turin, and started his own musical group: the Asternovas Orchestra.

Buscaglione already knew Renato as a friend and musician, and at that time, Fred needed to replace his pianist, so he asked Renato if he could work with him. Renato agreed, although he was busy performing in another venue. When he finished his work, he went to play the piano at the Buscaglione show, sightreading the score, causing Fred to admire him even more. When his contract ended in Turin, Renato returned to Viareggio to perform at the Gatto Nero with his S-13 orchestra.

Buscaglione went to see him in Viareggio, and asked him to be the pianist on his new tour in Holland. Uncle Renato had always had a fondness for windmills, so he signed the contract without even asking what his compensation would be.

When they returned from Holland, the group performed in various locations in the city of Turin. One of these was the famous Night Club *Il Faro* (The Lighthouse), which included—among its regular customers—leading personalities of Italy. The famous president and principal shareholder of Fiat, Gianni Agnelli (frequent customer of *Il Faro*), rented the premises on several occasions and hired the Asternovas Orchestra for private shows for his family and friends.

Soon, Giulio, too, had the opportunity to be hired by Buscaglione as the band's clarinetist, and he joined them. From then, the two brothers were part of Fred Buscaglione's Asternovas.

The group also toured performing in a series of nightclubs of various cities in Italy and Europe for several years.

At Fred and Fatima's wedding also attended his Asternovas Orchestra: (Left to right) Guagnini, Renato and Giulio Salani, the Buscaglione couple, Gastone Parigi and Cesare.

The Asternovas Orchestra by Fred Buscaglione, with Fatima Robins, at the Sanremo Municipal Casino.

With his versatility in many musical instruments, uncle Renato plays the double bass in the previous picture.

1950, Fred Buscaglione, Giulio Salani, Fatima Robins and Gastone Parigi.

*Beautiful years, all four of us have spent
me, Alma, Giulio, and Nancy, what a passion!
Touring all over Italy
with Buscaglione's orchestra.*

*From Rimini to Sanremo, then to Lucerne;
we played in almost all the casinos.
Geneva, then Lugano ... even in Bern
but this arrangement suddenly stopped...*

Fred soon began to play a character on stage that resembled an American gangster. He wore a look inspired by Clark Gable and other actors and characters from American films of the time (as well as the characters from books by Damon Runyon, one of his favorite authors): a double-breasted jacket, a mustache, and wide-lined hat.

Fred Buscaglione in his gangster attire.

During this time, the songs that Fred Buscaglione composed became famous throughout Italy; some of them were performed in partnership with his wife, Fatima Robins. They were: *Che bambola, Teresa non sparare, Eri piccola così, Love in Portofino* and *Whisky Facile*.

In an interview in 1959 for the historic newspaper "Stampa Sera" Fred said, "I've become famous too late ... for twenty years I've been playing in nightclubs and dancing halls." However, it was just in time to build his reputation and become one of Italy's legendary icons of the entertainment scene.

Unfortunately, it all ended suddenly with a terrible car accident on February 3rd, 1960, in which the singer lost his life. But, like so many legends who are taken too young, Fred Buscaglione is destined to never die.

On the site www.4loveofmusic.com you can listen to the songs: *Buonasera Signorina* and *Whisky Facile*, masterfully arranged by Renato Salani and interpreted by Giulio Salani.

Chapter 21
IN VENEZUELA

One morning in 1955, while Renato was still playing with Buscaglione's orchestra, he received two letters: one from the conductor of the RAI (Italian Radio and Television) orchestra, Giulio Razzi, offering him to be the director of the RAI singing school in Rome; and the other from his friend Alberto Franchi, a violinist from Turin, with whom he had worked for three years in Switzerland, offering him a six-month contract in Venezuela as pianist for his orchestra.

Two letters arrived almost together,
offering me two jobs in two interesting places:
I thought about it, I appreciated it very much
I didn't want to make the wrong decision.

In the City that tames its horses (From the
"Hymn to Rome")
Razzi offered me a singing school;
it is definitely a nice place, Rome,
but Caracas ... it has such a charm...!!!

*It is Franco the one who writes to me
and he is a friend,
bad things he would never do.
Do you know Almetta what do I tell you?
I'll bring the money back, eventually.*

*Therefore, with a mixture of fear,
enthusiasm and curiosity,
I decided to try the adventure
that introduced me to this city. (Caracas).*

Franchi's contract had many perks, so Renato agreed to be his pianist. He was thinking of staying only for a short time in Caracas, and the prospect of this new experience whet his curiosity. He was also keen on living in Venezuela, as it is close to Brazil, his country of birth, and one he was very eager to get to know better eventually.

Renato made his debut in Caracas at a restaurant called Normandy.

> **"EL NORMANDY"**
> "Hoy 6 de Enero - Reyes"
> **GRAND DINER DANSANT**
> Amenizado por el CUARTETO DEL MOMENTO - Con el
> Profesor RENATO SALANL
> Atención Maitre ALFRED.
> Plaza Morelos - Los Caobos.   Telfs.: 552393 - 550721.

This is a newspaper advertisement for the Normandy Restaurant.

He played there for six months, which passed very quickly, and, at the end of his contract he signed another one right away (without returning home) as the bar pianist at another restaurant, Tony's, located in Caracas at Plaza Venezuela.

From Normandy, I changed to Tony's,
our dear friend Tony Grandi,
who had a restaurant, the finest in town,
with the best crew under his commands.

A wonderful team that nowadays
you can't find anywhere, not even remotely ...
Today, some are in heaven, others in hell
and we're playing music ... my recollection of the
time, so vivid.

*Some of them I remember very well,
others are very rare for my memory;
they learned from Tony class and appearance,
he is the best night club owner ...*

Renato was happy with his work in Caracas and, having seen success and the appreciation of his audiences and fellow musicians, he decided Alma should join him there. She didn't hesitate when he wrote her a letter: she had been waiting anxiously for him to tell her to join him in Caracas—she was eager to hold her husband in her arms again!

*Yes, I was very happy for the opportunity,
there was a future, one could hope for;
but I was missing Alma for breakfast,
lunch and dinner, what should I do?*

*I wrote to her: Almetta come, I'm waiting for you,
however, do not delay, flee;
it's more than a month since I last made the bed
and I want to eat a salad.*

Do you know why I say this?
Because we never went to a restaurant,
    Franco made spaghetti with pesto every day
    and I was washing dishes ... how exciting!

    I never knew how to fry an egg;
    the risotto I made was fatal.
    It's obvious: I had to wash dishes and shut up,
    because I'll never be a real cook.

One evening Tony's restaurant hosted the famous Italian singer Katyna Ranieri, who was on tour in South America. Tony Grandi, the owner of the venue, introduced her to Renato, knowing that he had written the song Ranieri had sung at the Sanremo Festival in 1953: *No Pierrot*. Katyna enthusiastically agreed to sing it for the restaurant's audience, accompanied at the piano by Renato.

(Left to right) Katyna Ranieri, Ms. Giuliana (Tony's wife), Katyna's manager, Tony Grandi, and Uncle Renato in 1957.

After a few months, Tony had the idea of featuring gypsy music played in the cellar of his venue. Renato recommended two violinists: Giulio, his brother, and Vinicio Callegaro, the first violin in the orchestra of the *Teatro La Fenice* in Venice—a friend and colleague he knew from working in Switzerland. Giulio was still in Italy when he received Renato's call, so he finished his previous contracts, and moved to Venezuela to join Renato with Nancy and Leonardo, their eldest son.

237

Here they are disembarking from the ship at La Guaira Harbor in Venezuela.

Very soon the new band was formed. They played a prevalently Romanian-Hungarian gypsy repertoire; a kind of music genuinely enjoyed by the three musicians and by the audience. Callegaro, with his superb technique, made their show very exciting.

Renato, Giulio, and in the foreground, Callegaro.

Giulio playing the clarinet with Renato on the piano, Callegaro on the violin, and you can see the owner of the club, Tony Grandi, having fun playing the double bass.

Renato, Giulio, and Tony Grandi.

Tony also had another nightclub called the Key Club, but in those days, it was not very crowded. To attract customers, Tony asked the Salani brothers to perform there. For that occasion, Renato decided to form a quartet with him at the piano, Giulio on the violin, clarinet, and saxophone, Valdel Desiderati on the drums, and Pino Farruggia on the electric guitar. In only a short time, the Key Club became by far Caracas's most popular venue.

Renato Salani's quartet at the Key Club.

After their contract at the Key Club ended, the Salani brothers received a very interesting proposal from Mr. Jack, the French owner of the restaurant-nightclub, La Chismosa. Livening up the evenings with their music and their contagious spirit, the four musicians briefly made La Chismosa the favorite place of famous and influential people, including the President of the Venezuelan Republic in those days, Raúl Leoni.

*[...] Then we went to play at "La Chismosa"
and all the Venezuelan Elite
followed us in a flash, wonderful.*

*That place, about to be smashed up,
never dreamed of seeing so many people.
Mister Jack thought, "I'm a CHAMPION!"
I saved the club from closing.*

Chapter 22
The HIPOCAMPO

In Caracas, the Salani brothers had created their own loyal following. Wherever they went, everyone would enthusiastically go to see them so in 1963, they decided to open their own nightclub. The "Hipocampo" (Sea Horse) was born in the central area of Caracas, in a basement, below the Altamira Theater.

The Hipocampo Night Club in Altamira.

To decorate the walls of Hipocampo, they called a great friend and master from Viareggio, the painter and sculptor Beppe Domenici. This artist, who in his youth had been brought to light by making allegorical floats for the Carnival of Viareggio, was at that time famous for his wood, ceramic, and bronze sculptures. He had even worked at Cinecittà (the largest Italian film studio), creating the monsters that Goliath and Maciste fought in hugely successful films. In the Hipocampo, he made works of priceless artistic value, including a bas-relief seahorse that stood out from the wall of the ballroom, and a series of panels telling the story of *música criolla* (typical music of some Latin American countries, such as Peru and Venezuela).

Here, Uncle Renato describes Giulio during this new phase of their life in Venezuela:

We worked very hard,
with discipline, love, and perseverance;
we laid good bases for the future,
hoping we were on the right path.

Giulio is worried and generous,
kind, sincere and a good man;
honest to the point that you even get nervous,
he accepts the lightning but rejects the thunder.

Every hostile noise harasses him
this way, he tries to relieve the pains of others;
he cannot see sad people,
friends with problems go to him and ask for help.

And he does everything for God's love,
to show gratitude to God
for the talents that were given to him
as faith, ability, health and science.

He was always ready to agree
if it's for other people's convenience;
with kindness, in a good manner he announces
sharing his happiness with everyone.

Giulio, today, is still exactly the same;
in feelings .... a true gentleman.
A truly outstanding personality;
shouldn't I know it .... to tolerate Renato ...!

What a success! How many people!
What an emotion!
Fantastic joy remembering it;
there was the best of a generation,
everyone in Caracas wanted to visit it.

The staff, in a good way,
waiting with class until morning;
first of all, our cashier
with her royal appearance, because she is Regina.
(Her name means Queen in Italian)

Customers sent postcards
to remind us, to be remembered,
from Moscow, Baghdad, the Philippines
... they filled a whole wall in our venue.

The Salani brothers in their Night Club Hipocampo. Renato playing the piano and Giulio the violin.

In 1965, Renato Salani and his orchestra performed live during the filming of various scenes in the Mexican movie *Me ha gustado un hombre* with Tere Velázques and Julio Alemán. *Frágiles Palabras* is the title of the song composed by Renato and sung by the movie's leading actress, Tere Velázques.

You can listen to it on our website: www.4loveofmusic.com performed in Spanish by "Renato Salani y su Combo" as well as with the interpretation of Katyna Ranieri of Fragili Parole (in Italian).

Renato and Giulio also appeared on several television shows: at Radio Caracas Televisión, where the Salani band participated in Renny Ottolina's show, *El Show de Renny*, and at Venevision, where they performed several times in the *Sábado Sensacional* program with Amador Bendayan.

Giulio and Renato Salani at *Radio Caracas Televisión*

In the following pictures, the Salani brothers at *Sábado Sensacional* live show. Here with host Amador Bendayan.

Giulio Salani with Luís Alfredo Arévalo (above) and with Renato Salani (below), performing at *Sábado Sensacional* live show.

The Salani brothers with TV host Amador Bendayan.

Renato Salani y su Conjunto: (from the left): Renato, Luís Alfredo Arévalo, Peppino Mascoli, Nicola Ridolfi, Aldo Donà, Giulio and Nerio.

Giulio Salani.

In 1967, after four years from the opening of the Hipocampo Night Club, Caracas was struck by a violent earthquake. The building where the Hipocampo was located received so much damage that it was declared unsafe. As a result, the Salani brothers had to move their nightclub elsewhere. The owners of the Chacaito shopping center invited them to open a new Hipocampo there, knowing they would bring excellent music, an affluent audience and thriving nightlife to their venue.

For the decoration of the new Hipocampo, Uncle Renato went to Italy to again contact their beloved artist and friend Beppe Domenici. Beppe worked for six months on the project, sketching the designs, and creating his masterpieces. He took care of the whole project and created truly extraordinary artwork for the new venue!

On Valentine's Day, February 14th, 1968, the second Hipocampo nightclub celebrated its grand opening.

Here is the photo of Renato Salani's Orchestra in their Carnival costumes in front of the main entrance of the new Hipocampo in the *Centro Comercial Chacaíto*: (from the left) Peppino Mascoli on the drums; Pepe Castro, singer; Aldo Doná, singer; Renato and Giulio Salani; Harry Planchart at the guitar; and Tony Di Roma at the doublebass.

Each night, three bands performed, rotating shifts until early morning. The first band was *Renato Salani y su Conjunto*, with a repertoire of international music ranging from European (Italian, Spanish, American, and French) songs to Romanian-Hungarian gypsy music, with violin and piano.

Ciccio Barbarossa Orchestra was the second, and they played more Latin music, such as boleros, salsa, samba, cha-cha-cha, merengue, and bachata. The last band, Los Memphis, provided music to the younger crowd, playing more modern and popular songs of the moment included in the hit-parade.

In addition to the core musical groups, the Hipocampo featured internationally renowned artists for special events.

Among the performing artists were Aretha Franklin, Luciano Tajoli with Luciano Maraviglia, Albano Carrisi and Romina Power, Riccardo Cocciante, Gianni Bella, Nicola Di Bari, Sammy-Davis Jr., Frank Sinatra Jr., Sound and Company, Mariano Mores with his orchestra and dancers of Argentine tango, Eliana Pittman with the Carnival of Rio de Janeiro, the Cuban comic Álvares Guedes, the Spanish artists Sandro and Rafael, the Mexican Juan Gabriel, Rocío Durcal, Hector Cabrera, Delia, Peret, Julio Iglesias, Rocío Jurado, Camilo Sesto, Perucho Conde and Simón Díaz, the famous songwriter of *Música Llanera Venezolana*: typical music of the Venezuelan plain, played with a *cuatro*—a smaller guitar with four strings—maracas, and *arpa llanera*—a small harp.

Newspaper advertisements of the shows.

Ciccio Barbarossa's orchestra, with Giulio Salani playing the clarinet in Eliana Pittman's show.

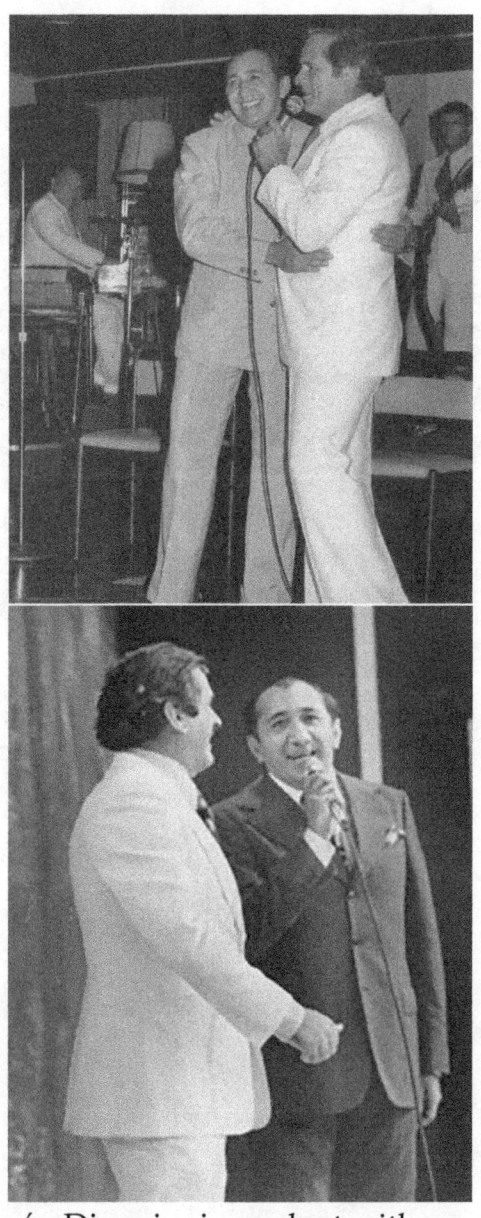

Simón Diaz singing a duet with my father,
accompanied by Renato Salani's Orchestra.

Domenico Modugno, an old and dear friend of the Salanis, and Giulio during a visit to the Hipocampo.

...and with Renato.

You can visit www.4loveofmusic.com to listen to a song composed by Domenico Modugno, masterfully arranged, performed by Renato Salani's Orchestra and sung by Giulio Salani: *Libero.*

In addition, the Hipocampo hosted an eclectic mix of parties and dances: sweet 16 balls (although in Venezuela girls commonly celebrate their 15th) birthday parties, graduation and wedding parties, corporate events, Christmas parties, New Year's Eve dances, Valentine's Day and Carnival masquerade balls, color themed parties as well as matinée performances of "Costume Children's Balls" organized for the benefit of the Venezuelan Foundation against Children's Paralysis.

GRAN BAILE DE CARNAVAL
PARA NIÑOS
A BENEFICIO DEL
HOSPITAL ORTOPEDICO INFANTIL
EL DIA 8 DE FEBRERO DE 1970
DESDE LAS 4 a las 7 p. m.

EN EL
HIPOCAMPO

TODOS LOS NIÑOS DEBERAN IR DISFRAZADOS
BAILES - JUEGOS - COTILLONES
PREMIOS A LOS MAS LINDOS DISFRACES

ENTRADA: Bs. 10.— Por persona
(Niños y acompañantes)

Mil gracias en nombre del HOSPITAL ORTOPEDICO INFANTIL

Children going to the Costume Ball at the Hipocampo.

Adult customers danced and enjoyed themselves until six or seven in the morning. As a child, I remember my father coming home from work when I was waking up to go to school. I would get ready to leave at 6:15 on the bus, and kiss my dad as he would arrive home. After long nights of entertaining, I could see that he was tired, yet he was still happy to have spent the night providing MUSIC and cheer to so many people.

And now I share with you the verses Uncle Renato dedicated to me when I was born:

*Almost one month since Alma
had come back with our three sons,
and Nancy too, was hospitalized
because her pregnancy came to fruition.*

*Really, she was also impatient
to get rid of that encumbrance,
she urged to present to her people
Barbara's cry or her trill.*

*Barbara, Barbaretta, Barbarina,
to express my affection, my heart does not cease,
for mom and dad, you are the Queen
for the entire Clan Salani, our Princess.*

*I believe your dad went crazy
when he saw you smile from the cradle. [...]*

From the left, Leonardo, my older brother, dad, and me.

In the meantime, as I'm writing these lines, Barbarina is living her fifteen years of the grain of life among the wheats; she is spreading her youth.

Good, beautiful, nice and scholarly educated,
arranges her life her way, her style;
as of the piano she is already a virtuoso,
Dad will buy her a new Steinway.

Precisely on my fifteenth birthday, my father gave me a baby-grand piano that I still worship as a precious jewel: a Steinway & Sons, built in Hamburg, which soon became my dearest friend. I care for and love it like a diamond, only allowing my best students to play it!

On March 21st, 1976, we had the pleasure of celebrating Leonardo's 20th and my 15th birthday at the Hipocampo. It was such a memorable party, and most of our friends and classmates came. From the left: my younger brother Sergio, my mom Nancy, my older brother Leonardo, me, and my dad Giulio.

By the mid 1960s Renato and Giulio were at the height of their career. Often the brothers were invited to play at high society weddings and parties all around Venezuela: Tigre, Cumaná, Maracaibo, Ciudad Bolivar, and others.

Life magazine in Spanish, on May 26, 1966, published the following article:

TWO ITALIAN BROTHERS SET THE TREND AND TRIUMPH IN A NIGHTCLUB.

In a city where is well known that nightclubs have a short life, the Hipocampo owned by the brothers Renato and Giulio Salani, not only survives, but also flourishes. The secret lies in their good music, the great number of people who return to enjoy themselves and the enthusiasm of their owners. Renato arrived to Venezuela from Italy in 1955 and worked in several clubs. After a while he called Giulio and together founded the Hipocampo in 1963. They established their roots in the New World and in particular in the eternal Springtime of Caracas...

Renato Salani, playing the piano and keyboard at the Hipocampo.

Giulio Salani playing his tenor sax.

Now I introduce to you some "secrets" that Renato has revealed to Venezuela Gráfica's journalist José Emilio Castellanos, during the interview of June 11th, 1967.

Castellanos: There is no one who has had fun in Caracas by night and does not know the orchestra of Renato Salani. Renato himself confesses that his ambition is to fascinate the audience while listening to their music, to make them reach the ecstasy.

Salani: We play everything the audience likes, and we are not in favor of a popular melody or another, if it is a melody that the orchestra does not like, I make a personal arrangement, until it reaches the desired goal.

Castellanos: And what is this goal?

Salani: The important thing is that people forget their problems and enter this world of musical passion. To distract listeners from their worries, we gradually make them enthusiastic about our musical interpretations until the whole audience is euphoric. Then the true party starts.

Renato states that it is necessary to preserve a kind of "special sense" or spirit of the moment, especially in order not to leave interruptions between the interpretation of one song and the other.

"It is essential not to separate a melody from another, otherwise those who dance will cool down and all the euphoria and dance dynamics are lost. In the arrangements, I join different melodies in a sort of potpourri."

Renato Salani's orchestra is complemented with instruments that can simultaneously serve either as soloists or as accompaniment, such as saxophone, violin, clarinet, organ, drums, piano, guitar, bass and, as far as the voices, all members sing as soloists, but always with the support of the choir.

"There are no stars among us, rather the orchestra becomes a Solar System where everyone has their role to make the music shine."

Every melody is good for Renato Salani, it all depends on putting a "proper stamp" in the arrangement. A waltz or a cha-cha-cha blend in his potpourri. But the selected songs depend on what the audience likes to listen to. Renato noted that on Sundays most of the customers are Italian. On Fridays, Venezuelans fill the venue, so that "criollos" rhythms are performed, while Saturdays are for "intercontinental euphoria".

"The important thing," says Salani, "is to make everyone understand how to get into the music, leaving out all obstacles. There is a moment when dancing the Compostela, where all those on the dance floor accompany the songs of the moment by making a train: kneeling and rising, in a fun group dance. No one in the club escapes this dance.

Among the most successful songs in his twelve-year Venezuelan career are: *America*, which has certainly reached the apex of popularity, along with *Guarda che Luna* and other famous songs.

Renato Salani's orchestra consists of six musicians, among which his brother Giulio is the most versatile. In the same set he plays the saxophone, clarinet, violin, flute and also sings melodies for lower, baritone voice.

The other members of the group were Valdel Desiderati, drummer and singer; José Rivero, guitarist and singer of bossa nova; Tony Di Roma, bassist, and a new acquisition, Manolo Mercerón, guarachero (expert in popular guaracha).

A few years later, in 1975, the magazine *Ve Venezuela* dedicated an article and front cover to Giulio:

Giulio Salani on the cover of the Spanish and English magazine *Ve Venezuela*.

THE ECONOMIST BECAME AN ENTERTAINER

There have been cases of visitors to Venezuela who delayed or postponed their return home in order to spend some more evenings at Hipocampo. It's true: many tourists are surprised by the lively and pleasant atmosphere of the nightclub.

As popular in its home of the Chacaito shopping center, as well it was years before, in the basement under the Altamira Theater, the club boasts an extraordinary success for its lifetime in the changing world of Caracas nightlife. How has it maintained its popularity? What's behind the years of success? We decided to ask singer and clarinetist Giulio Salani.

"Well," he said, "there are various reasons, such as the fact that we really like our job, that we work with enthusiasm and seriousness ... and another thing that helped me was my business and economics studies."

Now there is something new ... a musician who studies economy? Therefore, Giulio explained to us how everything started. He was born in Italy to a family of musicians. His father studied and graduated from the Conservatory of Bologna and their house was always full of music. His father, however, opposed the fact that his children became professional musicians and wanted them to be economists.

Renato, who at the age of 14th had an orchestra of 40 musicians for whom he made the arrangements, strongly refused. Instead, Giulio respected his father's wishes and began his studies at the University of Pisa.

In the post-war period, jazz swept the earth as a fever. The Salani brothers played at night, studied during the day and after work they met with other musicians to relax in a good jam session. Giulio talked about Renato affectionately, he always considered him more than a brother, a friend, a father, a counselor, a protector.

The Salanis and all their jazz friends dedicated themselves by investing time and money to present to the Italian and European public a spectacular, extraordinary show [...] but they could not afford a financial flop, they had to pay their debts, their mortgages to banks. The Salani brothers initially took their own way, sometimes playing together, sometimes separately, in Italy, Switzerland, Germany, Holland, etc. Giulio went on studying with firmness, supporting the exams between one contract and the other.

When he finished his studies, he married his great love Nancy and worked as an economist at a bank in Milan. But there was something terribly important that was missing in his life, and it was MUSIC. He kept his clarinet in the car so that after work he could play at night in some club or bar.

Finally, after two years, his wife Nancy encouraged him to go back to the band's life: "If you enjoy playing so much, why don't you go back to music?" Change came quick and fast: it was enough to send a telegram to Fred Buscaglione, and Giulio was happy again, his music colleagues were good and it was a joy to play with them ...

In 1957 Giulio signed a contract with Tony, then in Plaza Venezuela, and arrived in Caracas. At Tony's he played with violinist Vinicio Callegaro and his brother Renato. What they made together was not just music, they created special and fun moments.

When he played in the orchestra with Renato, every instrumentalist had to learn and memorize arrangements, so they didn't have to read the scores. Giulio only needed a single note to understand which song was to be performed. The programs were improvised, exciting and amusing.

The repertoire that the orchestra performed was not just music, it was a lot of fun and a great show.

In Caracas, their success is due to the fact that they have been able to create a nice and pleasant environment with music. In addition, their affectionate, respectful and polite manner to their audience, has made them appreciated by their customers who feel at home in the Hipocampo.

(Hillary D. Branch, February 1975)

Life's article as well as *Ve Venezuela's* appropriately emphasized the lively climate that filled the rooms where the Salanis played, an environment they could create and preserve. Hipocampo, for example, had a code of ethics that all clients had to respect: men could not enter without a jacket and tie, and women had to be accompanied by a date; those who put up a fuss and caused a commotion were immediately led to the door. Only couples who dressed and behaved appropriately—with respect and cordiality—were accepted into the club, in order to maintain the club's good name. My father and my uncle were not exempt from this code: the staff was very attentive, and constantly checked that all customers were following their rules. As they say, it's better to lose one customer today to keep one hundred for years.

Clients greatly appreciated these rules. The President of the Republic, Rafael Caldera, also attended the Hipocampo and often called to reserve a table for his daughter and friends.

I remember enjoying a New Year's Eve party at the Hipocampo with the Italian entrepreneur Ferruccio Lamborghini, a dear friend of the Salani brothers, who was a regular customer, often accompanied by his son Tonino.

The Salani brother's music had even gained an international following: in Portugal, during a family vacation, Renato recognized one of his songs in the background music of the restaurant where they were dining. The owner, recognizing him, had put on the record Renato had given him one evening at the Hipocampo. What a nice surprise!

Above all else, Renato and Giulio have always been very devoted men of faith; they have brought to fruition the talents that God has given them, and they never forget to thank Him for all the gifts He has given, such as health, the opportunity to be in a career that made them happy, and two lifelong companions who shared their ideals and aspirations.

Alma and Renato Salani.

Nancy and Giulio Salani.

The Salani family with friends at the Hipocampo: (from the left) Tony Cattabriga, Alma, Gloria Sergio, Nancy, Renato, Leonardo standing, Giulio, Barbara drinking, Stefano, Andrea and Riccardo Salani.

Giulio and Renato Salani in their night club at the Hipocampo's birthday party.

Giulio, Nancy, Alma, and Renato at the Hipocampo.

Moreover, *Renato Salani y su Conjunto* recorded 13 records at 33 rpm.

Renato Salani's quartet while recording a long play in the recording studio.

One of the recordings by Renato Salani's quartet. The art cover is by the painter Manfredo Michetti.

Here you can see the leaflet that collects several of the *Renato Salani y su Conjunto* records.

You can find the most beautiful songs of the records by Renato Salani and his orchestra on our website: visit www.4loveofmusic.com

Chapter 23
MUSIC FOR LIFE

During a 1975 interview, Giulio was asked what his future aspirations were.

"To live a little quieter," he said, "to enjoy the free time with my family, in peace." He added, "After so many years of singing and dancing every night with furor and excitement, though beautiful and fun, what I'm really dreaming of is a holiday at the beach."

Renato and Giulio Salani at the beach.

In fact, in 1982, when Renato was 60 and Giulio 57, they withdrew from the night life. Giulio devoted himself to sports—swimming in particular—and kept a musical "workout" with all his instruments. Renato continued with compositions and arrangements, cultivated painting (which has always been one of his other passions), and resumed writing his DIARY.

Renato's arrangements and compositions increased more than ever after retiring, like an unstoppable, overflowing river. Music is fluid, an evanescent language—listening to it, we enter into another life, another time, even another dimension. Renato wanted to live in this dimension forever.

At that time, the two brothers enjoyed family life, supporting their children and grandchildren in their various pursuits. I find myself very fortunate to have chosen the path of a career in music, following in the footsteps of my grandfather Euclide, my Uncle Renato, and my father, Giulio. Uncle Renato was especially crucial in making my concerts successful.

Several years ago, in Italy, I had the pleasure of meeting the Argentine pianist Laura Helman, who became my beloved friend, and in 1990 we formed a piano duo. Uncle Renato composed and wrote several arrangements for us, which we performed at several locations in Italy and Europe. These pieces have garnered overflowing praise and approval from audiences and critics alike.

Piano Duo Laura Helman and Barbara Salani in Concert at the *Antiche Terme di Massaciuccoli* with Maestro Renato Salani.

Laura Helman, Maestro Renato Salani, and Barbara Salani, after a concert at the Puccini Theater in Torre del Lago (LU).

Among the compositions Uncle Renato wrote for our piano duo (Duo Helman-Salani) is *Fantasía Venezolana,* which represents a collection of the most beautiful and famous Venezuelan melodies, reworked for piano four hands. This group of melodies has always been very well received and appreciated by all kinds of audiences. It moves those who perform it, and above all, excites those who listen to it. At the end of each of the performances of *Fantasía Venezolana,* the crowd erupts in cheers and applause, standing ovations, and *encore* requests.

At www.4loveofmusic.com website you can listen to Duo Laura Helman-Barbara Salani performing Renato Salani's *Fantasía Venezolana* for piano four hands.

Other compositions by Renato Salani that still have great success are: *Homenaje a Mariano Mores*, *La Cumparsita*, and arrangements such as the *William Tell Overture by* Gioacchino Rossini for two pianos, tangos like *A Media Luz* and many more.

You can listen to *Homenaje a Mariano Mores*, composed by Renato Salani and *La Cumparsita* by Matos Rodriguez, arranged for piano four hands by Renato Salani and performed by Duo Laura Helman - Barbara Salani at the website: www.4loveofmusic.com

The success of the *Fantasía Venezolana* was crowned on October 14th, 2014, when my brother Sergio and I had the honor of performing it with two pianos and the Symphony of the Americas, directed by Maestro James Brooks Bruzzese. The arrangement for two pianos and orchestra was composed by my brother Sergio Salani, based on Uncle Renato's original version for piano four hands. Once again, it was a huge hit.

Duo Barbara and Sergio Salani playing *Fantasía Venezolana* with the Symphony of the Americas, conducted by Maestro James Brooks-Bruzzese.

The complete version of *Fantasía Venezolana*, arranged by Sergio Salani for two pianos and orchestra, and interpreted by Barbara and Sergio Salani piano duo, with the Symphony of the Americas, can be found on the website as well.

Thank God, Uncle Renato was able to attend this concert, and enjoy the success and recognition of his piece.
This is the review by Lawrence Budmen published on Fort Lauderdale Connex.

"The Sergio and Barbara Salani Piano Duo was the concert's featured soloists and indeed the Salani family proved an indispensable part of the event with contributions from the pianists' uncle and father.

The brother and sister duo came together for Fantasia Venezolana by their nonagenarian uncle Renato Salani who was in the audience. Originally composed for piano-four hands, Sergio Salani arranged the score for two pianos and orchestra, the new version receiving its premiere. A distinctively classical medley of popular Venezuelan tunes, the piece contrasts elegant and sentimental melodies with throbbing rhythms. The Salani duo offered deftly coordinated pianism, bringing real Latin verve and bravura strokes to the finale, set to the famous Venezuelan melody Alma Llanera. The orchestral writing emerged warm and rich, the sections for winds and strings a standout."

-Lawrence Budmen

Unfortunately, two months after this wonderful event, on December 21st, 2014, Renato's heart ceased to beat—he was 92.

MUSIC accompanied him until the end. The day before he departed, he performed—with great agility and mastery—his favorite piece, *Clair de Lune,* by Claude Debussy. Alma, listening as usual with love and delight, praised the beauty of his interpretation.

Renato's departure has pained us all, but he generously gave us not only all of his scores and arrangements, but also the collection of twenty-two CDs, entitled *Renato Salani Yesterday and Today*, with all his beautiful compositions. We can still experience the beautiful moments of life together with him and his music.

His wife and three sons dedicated him the following epitaph:

Renato, prolific composer,
Exemplary man, father, and husband.
Music has accompanied you through all your lifetime
And with the Grand Staff (pentagram) staircase
You have ascended into Heaven.

Sadly, my mom, Nancy, left us as well in February 2012. We have many beautiful memories with her, enriched by all her love, her perseverance, and wise teachings. From the tours in Europe and Italy to the time spent in Venezuela, my mom always followed and supported my father, making him happy, and helping him face all the phases of life with joy.

Thank you, mother, for your generosity and the great support you have always given to your children and grandchildren. You've always been a great model of a mother and wife, and you were such an intelligent and refined woman. Mom, we miss you so much—dad remembers you and thinks about you every day.

To honor her and Uncle Renato's memories, I often go to the *Lady of Mercy Cemetery* in Miami where both urns are stored inside a glass enclosed reliquary.

A few years ago, my father, unfortunately, suffered a stroke as a result of a surgery he had undergone. Afterwards, he had difficulty speaking and he was so thin and frail that we thought he would not make it. The neurologists told us he would have to go through a lot of therapy and should try to regain his speech within a month—otherwise he would never be able to speak again.

Sergio decided to bring a battery-operated keyboard to the hospital, and each day I trained him for several hours with music therapy. Thanks to MUSIC—to the notes sung in solfege, the repetition of the words of songs he had known for so many years—with persistence, patience, and thanks to the devotion of the whole family, he managed to regain his speech and even sing again.

On this occasion, I realized that MUSIC really can do miraculous things! My dad has devoted all his life to music, and at the most critical moment of his existence, MUSIC repaid him by giving him his voice—his life, back!

Sometime later, my father was completely recovered, thanks to music therapy. Sergio and I had the honor of accompanying him on two pianos with the Symphony of the Americas, directed by Maestro James Brooks-Bruzzese, while he expertly sang in front of an audience of six hundred people at the Broward Center of the Performing Arts, Amaturo Theater in Fort Lauderdale, USA, ending with an enthusiastic standing ovation

From the left, with the Symphony of the Americas in the background: Barbara Salani, Giulio Salani, and Sergio Salani, while announcing the name of the song about to be performed: *Arrivederci Roma.*

Lawrence Budmen, in the online magazine Fort Lauderdale Connex, commented on this event with the following words:

"Repeated standing ovations for the Salani Duo brought a unique encore. Barbara and Sergio's father Giulio Salani was brought to the stage. The 89- year-old Italian crooner sang the 1955 Renato Rascel-Pietro Garinei-Sandro Giovanni pop hit Arrivederci Roma, accompanied by his children at the keyboards and the full orchestra. He sang with that authentic mix of throbbing sentimentality and easy, casual intimacy that is unique to the Italian popular song tradition. The Salani musical family is remarkable indeed!"

You can appreciate his performance on our website: www.4loveofmusic.com

MUSIC is still the thread of his life: he spends his days listening to all kinds of music, doing physical and musical therapy, playing his favorite songs on the piano, and of course, singing as best as he can. He is still able to stay awake all night singing, as he did in the old days! This is the only "blemish" he has, as it prevents sleep for those who would like to rest.

MUSIC is the language of the spirit. His current secret vibrates between the heart of the singing and the soul of the one who listens.
(Kahlil Gibran)

Having lived most of his nightlife singing, playing, and dancing, he happily believes that during the night is the best time to sing all his favorite music until dawn, singing as a reminder, recalling the love of his life…

Nancy … Nancyna …

Look at the moon…
Look, what a sea …
From tonight on
without you
I'll have to stay…

(In Italian) Nancy … Nancyna …

Guarda che Luna…
Guarda che mare…
Da questa notte
senza te
dovrò restare…

Guarda che Luna, composed by Fred Buscaglione, with arrangement by Renato Salani, performed by his orchestra and sung by Giulio Salani, is available on the website: www.4loveofmusic.com

BIBLIOGRAPHY

Levi, Primo. *Se questo è un uomo*. Einaudi, 1947[2]
Levi, Primo. *Ad ora Incerta*. Garzanti, 1984[3]
I heartily thank the heirs to the author and Garzanti Editions for giving me permission to publish the poem "Tramonto a Fossoli".
Ori Anna Maria, *Il Campo di Fossoli. From prison camp and deportation to memory place*, Carpi, Italy, APM, 2004.[4]
Pezzino, Paolo. *I crimini di guerra nel settore occidentale della Linea Gotica*.[1]
Rovatti T. *Sant'Anna di Stazzema* in «Millenovecento», No. November 25, 2004.[6]
Salani, Renato. *Diario*. (Unpublished).
Salvadori, M. L., *Contemporary Age History*, vol. 2, Loescher.
Schilling, Willy. *Kahla, Triangolo Rosso*, Geiger. 2002[5]

Zuccotti S. *Holocaust in Italy*, Mondadori.

SITOGRAPHY

http://www.museogotica.it/storia/
www.fondazionefossoli.org
www.primolevi.it
http://www.bolognatoday.it/cronaca/caserme-rosse-lager-bologna.html
http://curba.racine.ra.it/_static/materialeStud/olocausto/CAMPI%20STERMINIO.htm
http://www.colegiodante.com.br/ita/per-conoscere-la-scuola/100-anni-di-storia/
http://www.storiaxxisecolo.it/deportazione/deportazionecampi4.htm
http://digilander.libero.it/lacorsainfinita/guerra2/schede/campiconcentramentoitalia.htm
http://www.istoreco.re.it/default.asp?page=485,ITA
https://it.wikipedia.org/wiki/Guerra_di_liberazione_italiana
https://it.wikipedia.org/wiki/Potenze_dell%27Asse
https://it.wikipedia.org/wiki/Alpi_Apuane
https://it.wikipedia.org/wiki/Appennino_tosco-emiliano
http://www.iltorinese.it/notte-quella-notte-vita-breve-straordinaria-fred-buscaglione/
http://www.beppedomenici.com/it/biography/
http://memoria.comune.massa.ms.it/sites/memoria.comune.massa.ms.it

All photos found on the Internet and displayed in the book are of public domain.[7]

These are photos taken in Italy (or in Italian territory) and are in the public domain as copyright has expired. According to Law no. 633 and subsequent modifications, photographs devoid of creative character and reproductions of works of figurative art become public domain from the beginning of the following year following the 20th anniversary of the date of production (Article 92). According to the text of the law, such photographs are: "images of persons or of aspects, elements or facts of natural and social life, obtained by a photographic process or analogous process, including reproductions of works of figurative art and film frames. It does not include photographs of writings, documents, business cards, material objects, technical drawings and the like» (Article 87).

The images considered creative works of creative character, however, become public domain 70 years after the author's death (article 2, number 7 and article 32-bis).

Those pictures I'm using are from 1940s.

Chapter 12: THE CROSSING OF THE APENNINE MOUNTAINS:

Trying to get home, they crossed the Tosco-Emilian Apennines, a 59-mile trip across the snowy mountains [8]

(You can see all the distances hereafter with Google Maps)

https://www.google.com/maps/dir/Massaciuccoli,+Province+of+Lucca,+Italy/41027+Pievepelago,+Province+of+Modena,+Italy/@43.9842852,10.2902014,10z/data=!4m19!4m18!1m5!1m1!1s0x12d59be6333a0c3b:0x99e22b336d9ce087!2m2!1d10.3606548!2d43.8362144!1m5!1m1!1s0x12d55ffc0c2b6603:0x729e93a14893f095!2m2!1d10.5858786!2d44.1807864!2m2!1b1!2b1!3e2!4e1!5i1

From Pievepelago Uncle Renato walked to a neighboring town, Sant'Annapelago, to look for such guides. [9]

https://www.google.com/maps/dir/Pievepelago,+41027+Province+of+Modena,+Italy/Sant'Annapelago,+Province+of+Modena,+Italy/@44.1881708,10.5635168,14z/data=!3m1!4b1!4m14!4m13!1m5!1m1!1s0x12d55ffc0c2b6603:0x729e93a14893f095!2m2!1d10.5858786!2d44.1807864!1m5!1m1!1s0x12d560ea462c2b9b:0xcda95828d804f5cb!2m2!1d10.5524946!2d44.1919635!3e2

As did Gisto (a friend of theirs from Viareggio), he went to Tagliole, but neither of them found one. [10]

https://www.google.com/maps/dir/Pievepelago,+41027+Province+of+Modena,+Italy/Le+Tagliole,+41027+Province+of+Modena,+Italy/@44.1791827,10.5800333,14z/data=!4m14!4m13!1m5!1m1!1s0x12d55ffc0c2b6603:0x729e93a14893f095!2m2!1d10.5858786!2d44.1807864!1m5!1m1!1s0x12d561cbd5bc6579:0xafb9ce7ffb4514ca!2m2!1d10.6001266!2d44.1655164!3e2

On the morning of the third day of hunting for guides, my father went to Rotari, a village farther away. [11]

https://www.google.com/maps/dir/Pievepelago,+41027+Province+of+Modena,+Italy/Rotari+MO,+Italy/@44.1816391,10.5797748,13z/data=!3m1!4b1!4m14!4m13!1m5!1m1!1s0x12d55ffc0c2b6603:0x729e93a14893f095!2m2!1d10.5858786!2d44.1807864!1m5!1m1!1s0x12d561d452ca075d:0x6d37755a63e74e02!2m2!1d10.6166641!2d44.1657292!3e2

DISCOGRAPHY

Discover the musical works, videos, photos and information related to the book

MUSIC FOR LIFE
The Salani Brothers

By Barbara Salani

on the web-site:
www.4loveofmusic.com

Barbara Salani

Born in Caracas, Venezuela, from an Italian family of musicians, Barbara has pursued a life-long career as a piano teacher and concert pianist.

An alumni of the *Juan Manuel Olivares Conservatory*, Barbara graduated as Piano Professor under the guidance of Prof. Gerty Haas.

Later, she moved to Philadelphia where she graduated at the Philadelphia College of the Performing Arts (currently the University of the Arts) under the guidance of the famous concert pianist Susan Starr.

Barbara has performed as a soloist with several orchestras, including *Orquesta Filarmónica de Caracas, Orquesta Sinfónica de Maracaibo, New England Youth Orchestra* and *Symphony of the Americas*, who became her sponsor in the US.

She has participated in various radio and television programs and performed in countries around the world, including Venezuela, the United States, Italy, Spain, France and Greece.

In 1990, she met in Italy the Argentinean pianist Laura Helman, who became her dear friend and together they founded the Laura Helman – Barbara Salani Piano Duo.
http://www.duohelmansalani.com/

The duo has appeared in various Italian and European locations, obtaining a wide range of audience praise and critical acclaim.

In 2015, Barbara moved to Florida, USA, where she has been performing as soloist in recitals, as well as in two pianos and orchestra concerts with her brother, in the Barbara & Sergio Salani Piano Duo. Their performances have attracted the attention, approval and enthusiasm of critics and audiences alike.

As a piano teacher, Barbara is very esteemed as demonstrated by awards and student outcomes.
.

She has recently been appointed coordinator of Musicfor, a musical education project organized at Broward County's Boys and Girls Club. Musicfor is an international association founded in Switzerland for the support and development of music teaching in the disadvantaged areas of the world. Musicfor gives thousands of children the opportunity to move closer to music, expanding their perception of the world and gaining valuable new perspectives on life.

In 2017 Barbara wrote and published a book entitled *Music for Life*, (*Una Vita per la Musica*, translated in Italian and *Una Vida para la Música* translated in Spanish by the author) the result of years of research into the last century of her family's history.

The book tracks the story of her father Giulio and his brother, Renato, through their life adventures, first during their younger years in WWII and later in their musical careers through Europe and in Venezuela, sharing their talents and joy for music with all kinds of audiences.

CONTENT

Acknowledgments	3
Preface	6
Family Tree	13
1. Parents in Brazil	14
2. Arrival in Italy	27
3. Children working at Gatto Nero	40
4. World War II	47
5. During the war: historical background	58
6. The Salani family during war time: from displacement to imprisonment	71
7. Arrival at Fossoli	83
8. Testimonials of the survivors	91
9. Life in the Fossoli concentration camp	109
10. Nullo Viti	129
11. Kissed by Fortune	138
12. The Crossing of the Apennine Mountains	154
13. Giulio	162
14. Finally free!	169
15. The arrival home	175
16. The S-13 Orchestra and Trio Alba	183
17. Alma and Renato	204
18. The Sanremo Festival	210
19. Giulio and Nancy	213
20. Fred Buscaglione and the Asternovas	

Orchestra	226
21. In Venezuela	232
22. The Hipocampo	243
23. Music for Life	287
Bibliography	302
Sitography	303
Discography	307
About the author	308

Book Cover description:

Front cover:

The original toilet paper roll where Renato Salani wrote his *Diary* in verses while he was a prisoner at a Nazi concentration camp in Italy, during World War II.
In the background: the original music manuscript by Maestro Euclide Salani, Renato and Giulio's father.

Back Cover:

Pictures of their performances as musicians at the Hipocampo Night Club in Caracas, Venezuela: Renato (on the left) playing the piano and the keyboard, Giulio (on the right) playing the Sax.

Underneath, a 1944 picture when Giulio and Renato Salani were prisoners at the Fossoli concentration camp in Italy.